MUSIC THERAPY:
IMPROVISATION,
COMMUNICATION,
AND CULTURE

D1520712

MUSIC THERAPY:
IMPROVISATION, COMMUNICATION, AND CULTURE

By Even Ruud

Barcelona Publishers gratefully acknowledges the permission to reprint the following chapters in revised form granted by various people and organizations: Aalborg Universitetsforlag for Chapter 1; Eres for Chapter 2; the *Nordic Journal of Music Therapy* for Chapters 3, 4, and 7; Universitetsforlaget for Chapter 5; *Young* for Chapter 6; the editors of *Qualitative Music Therapy Research: Beginning Dialogues* (Barcelona Publishers, 1996), the *Music Therapy International Report,* and Pro Civitate Christiana (Assisi, Italy) for Chapter 7; the editors of *Levande Musikk* (Høgskuleutdanninga på Sandane), Universitetsforlaget, and State University of New York Press for Chapter 8; and Solum for Chapter 10.

This original book is published and distributed by Barcelona Publishers, 4 White Brook Road, Lower Village, Gilsum, NH 03448.

ISBN: 1-891278-04-5

First Barcelona Publishers printing July 1998

10 9 8 7 6 5 4 3 2 1

Copyeditor: Katharine O'Moore Klopf of 𝒦𝒪𝒦 𝐸𝑑𝑖𝑡
"Stone Circle" created by Bertha Rogers copyright © 1993
Cover photo of "Stone Circle" by Jamie Fishman copyright © 1995
Cover design and layout by Frank McShane

Printed in the U.S.A.

SOURCES

All the chapters in this book were previously presented at conferences or printed in proceedings or journals. Most of them have been modified, and some have been completely rewritten for the context of this book.

Chapter 1 is based on my keynote address at the Third European Music Therapy Conference in Aalborg in June 1995, which was printed in the proceedings, *Music Therapy Within Multidisciplinary Teams* (Aalborg, Denmark: Aalborg Universitetsforlag, 1996). Thanks to editors Inge Nygaard Pedersen and Lars Ole Bonde for permission to rework the material.

Chapter 2 was part of my doctoral dissertation in 1987 and was used as the text for a lecture I gave at the Sixth World Conference in Music Therapy in Rio de Janeiro in 1990. A version of this chapter was also published in German as "Der improvisierende Mencsh" in the second volume of *Musik und Kommunikation,* edited by Hans-Helmut Decker-Voigt, Johannes Eschen, and Wolfgang Mahns (Lilienthal/Bremen, Germany: Eres, 1988, pp. 202–210).

Chapter 3 was originally presented as a lecture for the Eighth World Conference on Music Therapy in Hamburg in July 1996 and was then published in the *Nordic Journal of Music Therapy* (volume 6, issue 1, 1997, pp. 3–13).

Chapter 4 is based upon my presentation at the Third Nordic Conference on Music Therapy, in Jyväskylä, Finland, June 12 through 15, 1997, and was published in the *Nordic Journal of Music Therapy* (volume 6, issue 2, 1997, pp. 86–97). Thanks to all editors and publishers for permission to use the material, especially Brynjulf Stige, editor of the *Nordic Journal of Music Therapy.*

Chapter 5 is partly based upon material from my book *Musikk og verdier* ([*Music and Values*] Oslo, Norway, Universitetsforlaget, 1996), although new material has been added.

Chapter 6 is a rewritten version of my article "Music in the Media: The Soundtrack Behind the Construction of Identity," published in *Young* (volume 3, issue 2, 1995, pp. 34–45) as well as of my lecture at the Nordisk forskerkongress in Oslo on June 26, 1992, called "Suburban Rock: Between the Global Music Industry and Local Cultural Production: (*"Drabantbyrock: mellom global musikkindustri og lokal kulturproduksjon"*).

Part of Chapter 7 was also originally presented in a workshop at the Sixth World Congress of Music Therapy in Rio de Janeiro, July 16, 1990. The article was later revised and published in the *Nordic Journal of Music Therapy* (volume 1, issue 1, 1992, pp. 21–29), under the title "On Research in Music Therapy: Metacritical Perspectives, Values, and Qualitative Methods" (*"Om forskning i musikkterapien: Metakritikk, verdier og kvalitativ metode"*). In that chapter, I have also included material from my lecture at the First International Symposium for Qualitative Research in Music Therapy in Düsseldorf, Germany, July 29–30, 1994, published as "Interpretation and Epistemology in Music Therapy: Dealing with Competing Claims of Knowledge" in *Qualitative Music Therapy Research: Beginning Dialogues*, edited by Langenberg, Aigen, and Frommer (Gilsum, NH: Barcelona Publishers, 1996). I also added material from my presentation at the Third European Congress in Music Therapy in Aalborg, Denmark June 1995, as well as from my article "Music Therapy as a Science: A Narrative Perspective," which appeared in the *Music Therapy International Report* (volume 10, 1996, pp. 10–11). The material was recently translated into Italian by Barbara Zanchi and published as *"Epistemologia e ricerca qualitativa in musicoterapia"* in *Emozioni e musicoterapia*, edited by Pier Luigi Postacchini (Assisi, Italy: Pro Civitate Christiana, 1997).

Chapter 9 is reprinted from *Listening, Playing, Creating*, edited by Carolyn Kenny, by permission of the State University of New York Press (New York, 1995). The material was originally given as a lecture at the First Nordic Conference in Music Therapy in Sandane, Norway, May 1–5, 1991, and was also printed in the conference's proceedings, *Levande musikk*, edited by Brynjulf Stige and Bente Østergaard. Then it was published in *Den påbegynte virkelighet: Studier i samtidskultur*, by Berkaak and Ruud (Oslo, Norway: Universitetsforlaget, 1992, pp. 136–162), with permission from the publisher.

Chapter 9 was originally a plenary lecture at the Sixth World Congress of Music Therapy in Rio de Janeiro, July 15 through 20, 1990, under the title "Music, Communication, and Improvisation." It has since been heavily revised.

Chapter 10 was prepared for a workshop at the same conference under the title "A Phenomenological Approach to Improvisation in Music Therapy: A Research Method" but was originally a part of my doctoral dissertation in 1987, which was published in 1990 as *Musikk som kommunikasjon og samhandling* (Oslo, Norway: Solum).

ACKNOWLEDGMENTS

Writing always makes an author visible in his or her profession. The process of clarifying my ideas that produced this book would not have been possible without extensive input from my colleagues and friends since the 1970s. First, I would like to thank my students, the Norwegian music therapists trained at Østlandets Musikkonservatorium, presently Norges Musikkhøgskole (the State Academy of Music), and at Høgskuleutdanninga på Sandane, for their patience when I have not stuck to my script and for their ongoing contribution to the dialogue process. At its finest, this teaching method resembles the best moment in a musical improvisation, the foundation on which we build our work.

I also thank to my colleagues and friends involved in the training courses, particularly Unni Johns and Tom Næss in Oslo and Brynjulf Stige at Sandane. Brynjulf provided many useful comments, critiques, and inspiring ideas, especially when he read a draft of this book.

In addition, I thank the enthusiastic group of music therapists who started their graduate training in the Department of Music and Theatre at the University of Oslo in 1994. Gro Trolldalen took on some of my administrative burden while this book was in the early stages. Trygve Aasgaard, my old friend and now a colleague, took over my teaching responsibilities for a year and initiated a new direction in music therapy in Norway, taking his values and broad range of musical and professional skills into somatic medicine.

On the Nordic scene, I thank Ingrid Hammarlund in Sweden for her long-standing cooperation and Kimmo Lehtonen in Finland for theoretical input and great moments of both humor and seriousness. Thanks to Inge Nygaard Pedersen, Tony Wigram, and Lars Ole Bonde, all at Aalborg University in Denmark, for including me in a promising international doctoral program in music therapy. Their generosity, organizational work, and exquisite hospitality in many an old Danish castle engendered inspiration and opportunities

to develop important themes in this book. I have also had the
pleasure of working with David Aldridge, who generously shared
his updated knowledge, research skills, and database resources.

Other Scandinavians who have inspired me at workshops,
as lecturers, and at social events include Mona Hallin and Anci
Sandell from Göteborg, Urban Yman from Stockholm, Nina Hol-
ten and Sören Mühlhausen from Copenhagen, and Claus Bang
from Aalborg.

There are many others, some of whom I met only once,
who have helped me clarify my beliefs, but as is often the case in
music therapy, the level of contact was deep. Some have become
friends, reminding me that my personal life is intimately connected to my professional one. Barbara Hesser at New York University, with the international networking she fostered at the
1982 conference on "Music in the Life of Man" and her participation in organizing the Phoenicia group, has always made New
York friendly. I have enjoyed the hospitality of David Burrows in
New York; he always reminds me that presence and time are two
of the most important factors both in life in general and in working out one's personal philosophy. Lisa Sokolov and David Gonzalez expanded my concepts of clinical practice, and I am grateful
for the exquisite musicianship they have brought to our field.
Clive and Carol Robbins have been my friends for years, and I
thank them for their persistence in carrying the ideas behind the
Nordoff-Robbins Institute further. (I was saddened recently by
Carol's death.) Of course, Paul Nordoff made a lasting impression
on me in his many visits to Oslo. Ken Aigen and Benedikte
Scheiby have helped me maintain a good New York–Scandinavia
link. The American contingent would not be complete without
Barbara Wheeler, who I first met all the way back at Florida State
University while in the master's degree program, which was
influenced by Donald Michel and Clifford Madsen, both of whom I
of course consider mentors. Later, I had the pleasure to get to
know Lisa Summer, who has done important work in installing
Guided Imagery and Music (GIM) in Norway.

I extend my thanks to all of you who have invited me to
exotic places. I remember with pleasure the hospitality of Lia
Rejane Barcellos and Alfonso Gonçalves in Rio de Janeiro. I thank
Yasuji Murai for the translation of my book *Music Therapy and
Its Relationship to Current Treatment Theories* into Japanese and

his invitation to come to Tokyo. There was Gabriella Giordanella Perilli in Rome and Elba, Gianluigi di Franco in Naples, Dorit Amir in Tel Aviv, and Chava and Eliezer Sekeles, who opened their home in Jerusalem to me. Ted Tims invited me to Minneapolis, and Mechtild Langenberg let me in on the important First Symposium on Qualitative Research in Music Therapy in Düsseldorf. I especially thank Johannes Eschen, who was behind the establishment of music therapy in Germany and organized an important international symposium in music therapy education in Herdecke in 1978. During these travels, I often met other music therapists and dialogued on music therapy and life in general. Thanks to Joseph Moreno in the United States for carrying the blues into music therapy, Leslie Bunt of the United Kingdom for his Music Space, Edith Lecourt of France for her books and the snails at the Café de la Paix, Charles Eagle for the Mexican restaurant treat in New York with Konrad Schily, to Cheryl Dileo for giving so much of her time to international networking, to Ruth Bright for her love of Norway and for expanding the field of music therapy into geriatrics, and to Gregorio Tisera for publishing my book *Music Therapy and Its Relationship to Current Treatment Theories* in Spanish. Although we met only once, I must include Susan Munro for her contributions to my journey through music therapy. I also thank the whole Phoenicia group, especially Helen Bonny and Sara Jane Stokes, who introduced me to GIM. Liz Broukhart and Chris Wildman made a particularly strong impression on me while I observed their work in Cape Town just a few months before the democratic revolution in South Africa; we could all learn from the way they made music therapy a part of a larger political and cultural context.

In Italy, I learned a great deal from musicologist Gino Stefani, who has taken a radical anthropocentric stand in musicology. I thank Barbara Zanchi of Bologna, who has helped me on several occasions as an interpreter and translator. I also thank Nora Cervi and the rest of the staff at the Pro Civitate Christiana in Assisi for their hospitality and for giving me the opportunity to speak to an Italian audience.

Sometimes our professional lives deeply intertwine with our personal and family lives. Thanks to Wolfgang and Beate Mahns for providing a safe year for my daughter in Hamburg and to Wolfgang in particular for editing and co-writing the *Meta-*

Musiktherapie. Thanks to all who have hosted me on study trips, often with my students: Alfred Schmölz in Vienna, Cybil Beresford-Pierce and Mary Priestley in London, and Hans-Helmuth Decker-Voigt in Hamburg. Thanks especially to Isabelle Frohne-Hagemann, now in Berlin, who came to Norway and who constantly reminds us all of music *as* psychotherapy. From outside the realm of music therapy, I thank Odd Are Berkaak for his input from the arena of creative and poetic anthropology.

Thanks to Østlandets Musikkonservatorium, presently the State Academy of Music in Norway, and the University of Oslo, both of which have provided space and often money for my sometimes too extensive travels.

My special thanks to Carolyn Bereznak Kenny, who had important input on the title for this book and invited me to Vancouver. I also thank her for editing many of my articles over the years, for our long friendship and intellectual exchanges, and for expanding the space for reflection in the field of music therapy. Thanks to Kenneth Bruscia for stimulating discussions, hospitality, and, most of all, for publishing this book.

Even Ruud
Florence–Oslo–Tjøme
January 1996–January 1998

PREFACE

This book grew out of a series of lectures and presentations I have given since the mid-1980s. It reflects my interest in the theoretical development of music therapy; in retrospect, "improvisation, communication, and culture" seems to have been the broad context within which I have worked. That context includes a preoccupation with music therapy and its relationship to broader health issues in society; a more politicized concept of music therapy; definitions and values connected to the concepts of *music* and *human being*; connections between music therapy and interaction and communication theory; the need for an emphasis on analytical, interpretative, and qualitative research in music therapy; as well as how discourse psychology and theory can help us reformulate our basic concepts.

These chapters further reflect my concern for the interdisciplinary aspects of music therapy in such fields as musicology, music and mass media studies, popular music and cultural studies, anthropology, and poststructural theory. I have tried to align music therapy theory with some broader postmodern theoretical currents.

The book's title suggests some key concepts that run through the whole book. Of course, music therapy is the main perspective from which the chapters were written. After I had chosen all the chapters, it became obvious to me that many of them are concerned with improvisation, which I see as the most important methodological tool in music therapy. Communication, another key concept, has crucial implications for music therapy. Embracing aspects of sharing and providing meaning, it touches on dialoguing and transmitting, interplay and coaction, and immediacy and intention as basic elements of human interaction. My core belief is that music therapy deals with meaning and significance in human interaction and musical experience. Over the years, I have also become convinced that any study of meaning has to focus on a particular situation within a particular cultural context. Culture, then, becomes the inevitable backdrop for therapeutic communication and improvisation.

CONTENTS

xvi Contents

Chapter 1

PATHWAYS TO
MUSIC THERAPY

In this introductory chapter, I will outline the process that led to the collection of my articles and essays into one book. By presenting in part my personal and professional background and my understanding of basic music therapy theories and the values behind them, I hope to make my position easier to understand. I will begin with my first interest in music therapy and trace the path to the present via three main routes, all intertwining and, I hope, creating some interesting crossroads. Some of my tracks may seem to be dead ends for some readers, and others may be real detours. Dead ends can show us where to go next; detours sometimes make life interesting, creating memories to be reflected on later.

The first of these routes concerns my involvement with the development of music therapy in Norway and my interest in it as a cultural enterprise, engendering a quest for its politicization. The second route begins with my training in music therapy at Florida State University (FSU) and briefly introduces some of the people, approaches, and ideas that influenced me along the way and led to my interest in a more interpretative approach, far away from FSU. The third route takes the reader through different stages of my theoretical development, from a preoccupation with developmental and cognitive psychology to communication theory, media studies, popular music research, and cultural studies.

Many of the ideas I present here are discussed more thoroughly in later chapters. I hope my story will illustrate that although we may think that what we believe at the moment represents some "truth," we live in a constant process that at best leads us to improved personal and professional understanding.

THE POLITICS OF
MUSIC THERAPY

To many entrepreneurial music therapists, the phrase *politics of music therapy* signals internal struggles and political fights over the right to define *music therapy*. Many music therapists have to fight against biomedical attitudes or other forms of one-dimensional paradigmatic thinking to gain respect for their work. In some cases, these struggles are rooted in personal antagonism; at other times, they are based on broader disagreements about how to define such concepts as *health* and *science* or about human values in general.

In this chapter, I focus more on this last aspect—on how music therapy can serve society's need for a more humanized concept of *health* and *quality of life*. Seen in this context, the history of music therapy in Norway may serve as an example.

The 1970s were the founding years of music therapy in Norway. After coming back from FSU as a Registered Music Therapist with a master's degree, I was at least formally equipped to start working clinically and to take part in the organizational work necessary to institutionalize music therapy in Norway.

I worked with Unni Johns, who had been trained by Juliette Alvin, Paul Nordoff, and Clive Robbins, and with Tom Næss, who was extensively trained by Nordoff and Robbins both in Norway and at the 1974 spring course at Goldie Leigh Hospital in London. We had a broad range of theories and methodologies from which to start. With help from pioneers of music therapy, we were able to pull the discipline in one direction. This lead to the establishment of the first training program in music therapy in Norway in 1978, of which I was the first coordinator.

Without going into detail, I can say that the development of music therapy in Norway was in some ways dissimilar to the process I have seen in other countries, which was hampered by many ideological and personal struggles.

First, we joined forces with older and more experienced music therapists, accepting their clinical and experiential authority. Second, we had formal authority, as trained music therapists from abroad, to initiate our own path, without support or intervention from other professionals. Third, we adapted our foreign training to the culture and educational needs of Norwegian society. This meant linking music therapy with special education, which has a strong influence on the general educational milieu in Norway, and building a theory and practice of music therapy close to what seemed to be the official code of language in the educational and clinical fields in which we were working. The rhetoric of music therapy was thus adapted by the desire and need to be accepted by the general educational and health authorities.

Our efforts to fit into such a context reflected my concern that music therapy should work closely with the needs of society as well as serve both the individual and societal needs of our clients. Early on, I defined *music therapy* as an effort to "increase possibilities for action." This did not mean only directing music therapy to the individual needs of clients, trying to empower their developmental skills to increase their personal sense of agency. It also meant that because "possibilities for action" were often hindered by the larger structural barriers in society, I felt the need to establish music therapy as something that could meet the broader sociological and cultural needs of the clients. This meant that therapists could see themselves also as cultural workers, taking music therapy values and approaches into the community. This initiative was taken up, through developmental projects in a small Norwegian community, by some of the first music therapists we trained. Brynjulf Stige, together with Ingunn Byrkjedal and Mette Kleive, did important work in bringing the ideas and methods of music therapy to the local community (Kleive and Stige, 1988).

In the early 1990s, when large-scale reform in services for the mentally handicapped took place in Norway, music therapists worked hard to show how music therapy could be brought into the community, outside of institutions. Within a political context, this meant using music therapy to set up arenas for interaction among those threatened with isolation from the rest of the community. Networking through music groups, trying to open doors to society at large, became the goal of some music therapists. In Chapter 4, I explain in more detail what I mean by linking music therapy with a broader way of thinking about health. My key concepts there are drawn from the use of music as tool for encouraging participation, networking, opening doors, and empowerment through a strong musical identity.

Inherent in this therapeutic approach are some of the basic values and principles of music therapy—for instance, the use of improvisation and music dialogues to engage clients at their level of competence. With respect to cognitive, motor, or social competence, it means increased access to musical activity, via a flexible musical framework, so that all can participate in the music group at their own level of musical competence. The concept of musical dialoguing also means starting with the music cultural background of clients. My definition of *music* as a sign—as a communicative message with both inherent musical and extramusical or cultural referential qualities—means establishing musical interaction on the basis of the code competency of clients. In other words, clients have to master the language of music as a series of rules governing the perception and production of musical utterances. In working with severely disturbed handicapped clients, this might mean establishing the code within an individual session, restricting the code to a private domain. In group work, this might often require an awareness of folk or popular music traditions that constitute the musical identity of clients. An example of the latter is the use by Norwegian music therapists of rock group formulas.

A politics of music therapy thus aims at the more general empowerment of clients, in the sense of helping establish them within a community network. This is the solidarity aspect of music therapy. Building on respect for idiosyncratic musical identity, this means enhancing the personal dignity of the people with whom we work.

This sociologically inclined narrative of music therapy would not be possible without a foundation in some of the basic principles or approaches developed in the laboratory of clinical or creative music therapy. I have already mentioned improvisation and music dialoguing as some of the presuppositions for this work. Some of the more basic aspects of identity-building through music aim to establish a context for developing a sense of personal agency. We can see this in improvisational work with handicapped people who, through this mode, are given the chance to gain a sense of mastery through their actions, thus expressing themselves without using words. Within the discursive approach I adhere to, this does not mean revealing, awakening, or expressing any "true self" on the behalf of clients. Instead, it means helping clients constitute a place or a position in relation to themselves from which to act, to form a personal narrative that they feel in accordance with how they experience reality.

This stance would presuppose a sense of body, a sense of subjectivity. In political science, such aspects of self are often neglected. Politics has too long been identified with broader socio-logical themes, such as class struggle and economic policy. In the 1970s, we witnessed a focus on the "politics of identity," which meant that groups within society who were classified according to ethnicity, gender, sexual orientation, or—in the case of music therapy—cognitive abilities or mental health reclaimed their rights to individual freedom. Lately, a postmodern climate has extended this struggle so it has crossed categories of even gender or ethnicity, thus bringing acknowledgment that within such groups, there is individuality. For the field of music therapy, the politics of identity also means that people with cognitive or emo-tional handicaps have the right to choose between different mate-rial or cultural realities. All this has led to political recognition of the value of emotions and spirituality. Even the body has become a site of political relevance.

Such themes of "self-restoration" were recognized early on within the field of music therapy. The problem has been to rec-oncile preoccupation with such personal matters with a society and democracy whose economic policies or totalitarian forces make life difficult for groups and individuals.

Of course, music therapy does not do away with oppression and economic exploitation. Too often, music therapists make the leap to romantic and metaphysical stances to the effect that music (or therapy) can reveal the "true self" of the person or even cure society's disharmony. A politics of music therapy must come to terms with its limitations. It must recognize its interdependency with material and economic forces and align with those forces in society that work toward creating a space for human empowerment, self-insight, personal growth, solidarity, and social networking and with those that work toward alleviating structural forces blocking possibilities of action.

Recently, several authors have applauded Michel Foucault's statement in which he envisions art in the service of personal fulfillment:

What strikes me is the fact that in our society, art has become something which is related only to objects and not to individuals, or to life. That art is something which is specialized or done by experts who are artists. But couldn't everyone's life become a work of art? Why should the lamp or the house be an art object, but not our life? (Rabinow, 1986, p. 350)

Music therapists, along with other arts therapists, may increasingly come to see themselves as avant-garde in efforts to achieve this goal. For music therapists, music was never seen as something practiced in service of the art itself but as a means by which individuals can realize greater personal and social fulfillment.

I must add, however, that although individual fulfillment may seem an important source of health and well-being in our society, we should not forget how individualism has to be counterbalanced by a larger emphasis on the formation of groups or smaller communities. Music provides an important source of group belonging, and music therapists have the tools and knowledge to provide communal spaces for those who feel left out of society.

PROFESSIONAL INFLUENCES

European music therapists often now discuss the scientific status of their profession. *Science,* to many people, means to measure the effect of something, to establish correct or predictable procedures, to establish some kind of truth. When I talk about the importance of science for our profession, however, I want to underline the importance of establishing some way of talking about and discussing music therapy as a profession, as a field of theory and practice, or as a kind of metadiscourse. This metadiscourse, or rather metacritique, should enable us to maintain a rational dialogue about our ways of thinking about ourselves.

This understanding of science as a kind of metacritique, rather than as a way of establishing the truth value of music therapy practice, needs some historical context. When I began my training as a music therapist at FSU in 1971, I was immediately immersed in a scientific climate—that is, in the ideal of natural science transferred to the field of music therapy. This was evident in two ways: in the established E. Thayer Gaston tradition of music therapy as a university discipline, represented by my supervisor, Donald Michel, PhD, and in the newly established view of music therapy as behavior modification, represented by Clifford Madsen, PhD, which had a firm grip on the FSU training program at that time. The Gaston tradition meant, for instance, a basic natural science outlook on research in music psychology. It also meant the use of physiological measurement to register the experience of music, acoustical data on music to reveal the nature of music, and so on. This approach is evident in the first American standard textbook, *Music in Therapy* (Gaston, 1968). That such an approach was preferred at the time is of course clearly understandable in view of music therapy's marginal position as a new paramedical profession striving to be recognized by the larger scientific community.

Music therapy was not totally new to me, of course. Coming from the more idealistic and indeed charismatic influence of Paul Nordoff and Clive Robbins, I was familiar with the humanistic, improvisational, or what some might have called speculative tradition in music therapy. I hesitantly accepted my new "scientific" curriculum, carefully navigating between my new teachers and a useful library. I listened to lectures on acoustics and Skinner in the morning and wrote papers on phenomenology, Buber, Freud, and Zuckerkandl in the evening. If old files in the music therapy department at FSU still are kept, you might perhaps find some incomplete papers on Buber and the I–Thou relationship among all the "contingent use of music" articles.

One thing that I learned to accept and that probably has made a lasting impression on me was Professor Michel's Midwestern skepticism and the overall pragmatism that infuses the North American outlook on life. "I am from Missouri. I am a skeptic— show me," Professor Michel used to say, holding up his closed fist. I often remembered this when I met music therapy students and therapists who claimed some hidden truth or nature within music that would have an universal effect upon people. When I later undertook, as a part of my doctoral work, an extensive study of the history of music therapy, I constantly ran into narratives claiming some kind of metaphysical status for music (Ruud, 1980a, 1990a). Skepticism, or rather the tradition of Karl Popper, which claims that statements about reality ought to be made in a form that can be refuted, brings some sense to the field of music therapy, which still has believers in music's supernatural powers. We should constantly remind ourselves that our discipline is surrounded by lots of mystical, speculative thinking, especially in this New Age era. People and ideas that are not always concerned with standards of rationality keep gravitating to our profession.

Pragmatism keeps occurring to me as one alternative. When it has been so hard to establish "the truth," the pragmatic values of theories and explanations seem to be a way to deal with competing claims of knowledge, as I will discuss later.

In the years that followed my return to Europe—after I wrote the book *Music Therapy and Its Relationship to Current Treatment Theories*—some rather heavy issues bothered me. My book was based on my master's thesis in 1973 (Ruud, 1973a, 1980b, 1990b, 1990c; Ruud and Mahns, 1991) and was really an effort to solve the dilemma of being torn between different therapeutic or scientific schools of thought.

Going to the United States to study music therapy did not become the pilgrimage I had sought. FSU was the Mecca of the behavioral or positivist school of music therapy. On the other hand, it was one of the only institutions in the United States with a graduate program in music therapy that was also concerned about research in the field, and I surely was offered a great deal of hospitality, intellectual engagement, and personal care by my teachers.

In the years after FSU, I took several trips around Europe. I learned through my friends Unni Johns and Trygve Aasgaard of the more eclectic attitude of Juliette Alvin in London. Together with my friend and colleague Tom Næss, we visited Alfred Schmölz in Vienna and walked through the very same buildings where Freudian and Adlerian therapy began. I went to Paris and heard other psychoanalytic narratives from Edith Lecourt. We met with Johannes Eschen in Hamburg and tried to catch up with Mary Priestley's Analytical Music Therapy—that time, it was the Jungian version. One afternoon in Hamburg with Lilli Friedemann's group improvisation—she talked Swedish to us and served homebaked apple cake—made a lasting impression.

There were more in Hamburg. Isabelle Frohne-Hagemann showed us how to use receptive techniques combined with deep analytic work, and Hans-Helmuth Decker-Vogt invited 20 of us to his center in Lünenburger Heide to see videos of music therapy conducted in an adult clinical setting. Later, I was impressed with the new "Herdecke generation" of music therapists and learned more from Wolfgang Mahns, Inge Nygaard Pedersen, and Benedikte Scheiby about the value of the psychoanalytic approach in music therapy. All these trips, often with students but sometimes by myself, to congresses and symposiums all over Europe made me drift farther away from the positivist school of music therapy.

Although the behavioral approach seemed to solve some basic problems concerning measuring the effects of a certain music therapy approach, I was intrigued by the challenge of answering not only if and how music is effective, but *why*. I thought there would have to be an answer to the problem of the nature of music, some way to explain how music was constituted in order to function as a therapeutic means. I felt that the positivist approach—all the measurement of blood pressure and galvanic skin responses—said nothing about the individual's experience of music or about the structure of or meaning in music. I remember one passage from music philosopher Victor Zuckerkandl, who wrote critically about how the essence of the experience of music really could not be captured by a positivist researcher's measuring equipment, about how the richness and complexity of the mind really outplays machines. Instead, there might be a route to knowledge through phenomenological description or hermeneutic interpretation of music. These approaches were both hard to grasp and apply, and I struggled with their meaning for many years.

There was another challenge, not really dealt with in the North American scientific climate: critical theory, or the Frankfurt school of thought. Music therapy has a long history of claiming general cultural value by serving prophylactic purposes. Much contemporary music therapy seemed to have become too centered around the individual in an institutional setting, forgetting the surrounding society. Also, a lot of music therapy seemed to comply with repressive psychiatric practices sharply criticized from the

1960s onward by the antipsychiatry movement. It was a challenge for music therapy to both serve the community at a broader level and serve some emancipatory needs of the individual instead of becoming part of medically dominated psychiatry. Psychoanalysis and a radical social attitude, for some of us, had to be integrated into the expanding field of music therapy.

This was the 1970s. It was obvious that the traditional concept of science had become problematic for an interdisciplinary profession that tried to combine art and therapy, biological medicine and sociological critique, and concern for the individual as well as for the relationship between the individual and the surrounding community. Adopting the improvisational method so strongly advocated by Paul Nordoff, Clive Robbins, Alfred Schmölz, and Mary Priestley, to name some of the pioneers, created many problems for those who held a positivist or natural-science attitude, which meant using methods based on prediction and replication to establish a scientific truth. There is really no way to repeat a study based on musical improvisation, and it is just as hard to make methodological predictions based on the rules of improvisation.

There was a problem, though, with the somewhat idealistic and sometimes loose, speculative grounding of a great deal of music therapy theory and practice. I remember writing letters to Paul Nordoff and Clive Robbins advising them to move more explicitly toward humanistic psychology. Clive came to Oslo and lectured brilliantly on Maslow and music therapy and read from the Sufi stories after we had discussed the future of music therapy, reminding us that the wisdom in the art of music and improvisation is not so easily adapted to scientific discourse.

In Oslo, we established the first Nordic training program in music therapy in 1978. I increasingly felt the need to find a new theoretical base for music therapy, without leaving behind the idea of the art of improvisation. Remember that the Nordic countries had a strong tradition of music therapy in special education. Such pioneers as Claus Bang and Olav Skille made significant contributions to this particular field, so politically, it was the right move to align music therapy with special education. Jean Piaget and cognitive psychology seemed to be a good starting point in the effort to combine developmental psychology with aesthetic theories of music. From musicology, Leonard B. Meyer's theories of music and expectations proved to be valuable input in the therapy theory–dominated field. This constructivist approach to learning and interaction in music made sense when we tried to understand how children learn from their improvisations and how they use their skills to construct musical and personal identities as communication tools. The field of communication theory was a natural one to enter.

In the 1980s, we saw a gradual shift away from the dominance of positivism in music therapy. In 1982, Barbara Hesser invited music therapists from all around the world to partake in the New York symposium, Music in the Life of Man. Things had changed in the United States since I had traveled there 10 years earlier. A new organization, the American Association of Music Therapists (AAMT), had been initiated. Under the leadership of Kenneth Bruscia and Barbara Hesser, it was working to develop the neglected humanistic tradition in North American music therapy. In the context of the struggle between the National Association of Music Therapists (NAMT) and the AAMT, the New York symposium was a politically important move in reconciling the small group of humanistic music therapists, mainly from the East Coast, with a larger international community. Meeting with South American music therapists—for instance, Lia Rejane Barcellos from Rio—I learned that humanistic and hermeneutic traditions in European music therapy had much in common with music therapy from the southern hemisphere. At this symposium, I also met Carolyn Kenny, who had explicitly criticized the positivist dominance of music therapy in her thesis *The Mythic Artery: The Magic of Music Therapy* (Kenny, 1982). Later, she emphasized the theory-building aspect of music therapy in *The Field of Play: A Guide for the Theory and Practice of Music Therapy* (1989). Leading AAMT universities, such as New York University (Barbara Hesser) and Temple University (Kenneth Bruscia, Cheryl Dileo) sponsored doctoral research with an emphasis on qualitative methods. Increasingly, phenomenological and hermeneutic approaches were explicitly put to work in music therapy research (Amir, 1992; Bruscia, 1995a; Forinash and Gonzalez, 1989; Ruud, 1987; Wheeler, 1995). In Europe, Rosemarie Tüpker wrote books and articles on qualitative methods (Tüpker, 1988). The First Symposium on Qualitative Research in Music Therapy in Düsseldorf, organized by

Mechtild Langenberg in July 1994, represented an effort to gather some of these researchers and thus made a significant contribution to the development of this new approach to music therapy research (Langenberg et al., 1996).

This short historical narrative should help the reader understand how the field of music therapy came to be in its current multiparadigmatic situation within science. Science, however, is no longer occupied with finding a single truth, or even defining a single reality; I will elaborate further on this later. Together with the new paradigm of naturalistic or qualitative research, there is a growing acceptance that people interpret reality differently, that our life worlds inform our interpretation of music in a way that makes all concerns about universal meaning in music problematic. This situation could, however, stimulate us to revive long-forgotten speculative traditions within our field. The problem of competing claims of knowledge and interpretation demands serious attention.

THEORETICAL INFLUENCES

Looking back at my theoretical development, I see that my earlier and present positions may well be reflected in the lectures I have given during my 20 years in the music therapy program in Oslo. From the very beginning, we had a very favorable situation. The conservatory generously accepted our proposal for a program in music therapy that included several teachers of methodology, theory, and practice. Our plan to accept only six to eight students a year in our 2-year graduate program was also approved, which made it possible to give students individual supervision by trained music therapists in the clinic 1 or 2 days a week.

In the first years, I coordinated the program and taught theories of music therapy. Gradually, this subject was split into four courses: (1) introduction to music therapy, including definitions of *music, illness, handicap, health,* and so on, as well as functions of music in music therapy; (2) systematic musicology, comprising such subjects as music aesthetics and psychology, sociology, and anthropology of music; (3) theories of music therapy; and (4) ethics and the theory of science.

One of the first articles I wrote on music therapy was an attempt to align music therapy with developmental psychology (Ruud, 1975). The main argument was that "doing music therapy" had to involve and influence children's development in all areas: intellectually, socially, sensorimotor abilities, and emotional capability. Partaking in music had to involve the perception, emotions, body, and social awareness of the child—and the focus was clearly on the individual child.

In this connection, Swiss psychologist Jean Piaget's theory became useful in understanding how music therapeutic activities could involve children's sensorimotor capabilities—that is, develop their cognitive capabilities. Cognitive theory also helped explain the development of musical "ability." It seemed reasonable to think that some kind of musical competence is established in children while they are influenced by or making music: children assimilate the musical stimulation and accommodate their inner musical structures or schematas. This meant that emphasis was put on learning and cognition: having acquired a musical code or competence, children could be engaged in musical activities.

This understanding could be aligned with the concept of meaning and expectations in music as outlined by musicologist Leonard B. Meyer (1956). When we improvised with children, and if the improvisation was matched with the state of accommodated musical knowledge, we could trigger (musical) initiatives or musical responses necessary to establish a communication. Through playing with children's repertoire of expectations, we could engage them in meaningful musical conversations. This meant a move away from a belief in an inborn universal musicality in children, which sometimes could not sufficiently explain the richness of an improvisation.

This approach had some weaknesses, however. First, the cognitive emphasis underplayed the importance of body and emotion, although the theory of music and expectation told us that affect was aroused when musical expectations were fulfilled, disappointed, or delayed. It seemed to be a dynamic side of musical expression important to music therapy. Music has personal and symbolic significance, so its expressiveness, its link to personal history and to the body, and its symbolic meaning could not easily be recognized within these cognitive-theoretical frames.

Second, the psychodynamic approach clearly had to be investigated. Music had to be a carrier of symbolic meaning referring to inner states, perhaps unconscious, as well as to feelings related to the perception of self. As I explain in greater detail in Chapter 3, music seems to promote an awareness of feeling, body, and self that is a cornerstone of music therapy.

These problematic issues seemed to be oriented in one particular direction: the experiencing person. It seems more in line with current developmental theory to shift attention from the client as such to the interaction between client and therapist. Some music therapists have now changed their role from one of interacting directly with the client during music therapy to one of counseling other staff or parents who are involved in daily musical or communicative activities with the client. This reveals that what is going on in the client is as much a reflection of the interaction between the client and the other as of the developmental process. It seems more appropriate to focus as much on the adult's behavior—therapist's or parent's—as on the client's, or to focus on the *relation* between the people involved in communication. (My thanks to Gro Elisabeth Hallan Tønsberg, Tonhild Strand Hauge, Gro Trolldalen, Rita Strand Frisk, Randi Rolvsjord, and Rigmor Sæther in particular, who, through their research, have helped me grasp this new paradigm.) Counseling the parent to master communicative awareness appears to be the right move for music therapists because it seems to fit well with recently developed interaction theory, which posits that the child is a well-equipped communicator from the beginning.

In Chapter 9, I will discuss further how the use of interaction theory may be appropriate when we want to understand how improvisation can contribute to children's development.

TOWARD A NEW PARADIGM IN MUSIC THERAPY?

My theoretical development seems to have moved in the direction of an interpretative ideal, with influences from European hermeneutics and recent qualitative research. If we use the term *paradigm* loosely, it might be right to say that music therapy now is facing a radical shift in theoretical orientation. The emphasis now is not so much on measurement and quantitative studies; rather, we see an interest in qualitative research. Earlier mechanistic and organismic thinking is being replaced by a more narrative and discursive practice. New musicology, influenced by music anthropology and feminist and cultural studies, also challenges some of our underlying suppositions about how we understand the subject of *music*.

I am (painfully) aware that changes in theoretical orientation lead to changes in terminology, as is evident throughout this text. Readers may already have noticed my extended use of such concepts as *narrative, discourse, sign, code, constructivism, reflexivity, identity,* and the like. I am aware that I do not always manage to define these terms, although there are several instances throughout the book in which I elaborate upon them. I hope the contexts in which I use them will help readers understand my position.

One important element in this "hermeneutic" turn of events concerns our understanding of the very concept of *music*. I mentioned Meyer's theory of music and expectations, which meant an orientation toward explaining the meaning aspect of music, considering music as "a work" rather than a performative act. Because *improvisation* implies what we may term "musical orality," it seems today more relevant to find support in musicological theories that treat music not as an object but rather as a performative act. In other words, we must stress the importance of the signifying practice or how the context of the musical interaction is important to the formation of meaning in music (see Walser, 1995).

One of the problems we must struggle with is why music is effective as a therapeutic medium. If the answer is "because music creates meaning," we certainly create another question: How and why is music meaningful in therapy? Although Meyer provided a strong lead by directing our attention to the expectations aroused in us when we relate to music, there is more to the story when the subject is improvised music. When we improvise, we do not make explicit some hidden meaning embodied in the musical structure. The participatory nature of improvisation gives rise to a sort of meaning stemming from the dialogical nature of musical interaction. Ethnomusicologist Charles Keil redefined Meyer's "emotion and meaning" as "feeling and motion," thus opening the field for improvised performed music to a whole range of genres outside the Western classical canon (Keil, 1966; Keil and Feld, 1994).

This ethnomusicological turn in understanding how communication and meaning are established in an improvisation gradually grew out of my preoccupation with musical communication themes. In my music psychology lectures, I increasingly spoke about the societal and cultural influences on musical development. I felt it important to establish music communication on the learned code of musical competence, so I sought to trace how this code was established in children's everyday lives. This led me to investigate, in the mid-1980s, musical influences on children, especially those from popular music. I did studies on the repertoire of children's music, children's television programming, and youth culture and popular music. I soon found myself immersed in popular-music studies, writing books and articles on music videos. I met with a Norwegian anthropologist, Odd Are Berkaak, who was also preoccupied with rock music and youth cultures, and we obtained a large grant from the Norwegian Research Council to do field work among local rock musicians in a suburb of Oslo.

Being drawn to music anthropology, especially the trends emphasizing so-called performance theory, constructivist theory, and narrative theory, made me realize not only how deeply music is embedded in our culture and world but also to how great an extent it produces culture and transforms social organization. (In Chapter 6, I discuss this study and argue that music therapists may learn from and benefit from an anthropological understanding of music.) This in turn made me aware of the importance of context and all kinds of extramusical discourses when meaning is established in music. Anthropology also teaches us an important lesson about how "local" truths are more important than any claims of universality—how the way we tell the story about our reactions to music is a kind of "discourse," or a way of telling that gives local meaning to music.

Seeking deeper understanding seems to be a dialectic process. Recently, I have again come to see the challenge from developmental psychology—represented by Daniel Stern and Colwyn Trevarthen—which is to determine how biological forces interact with early development. This means we have to add to the story about musical communication how an aspect of immediacy in musical communication lays the ground for later cultural influence.

In trying to reconcile these many influences, from biology to anthropology, I found it necessary to study music and identity. For many years, I gathered musical autobiographies from my students. In analyzing these stories, I came up with a theory of the nature of music's contributions to the foundation of our identities, which is summed up in Chapter 3. This time, I was influenced by the current theoretical emphasis on reflexivity, which to me means to be aware of how our preunderstanding of a phenomenon informs our reading of the situation and our interpretations. Such a preunderstanding may involve our theoretical background, our cultural position, our choice of concepts and metaphors—in other words, our linguistic resources.

The most recently written chapter in this book (Chapter 4) concerns the issue of music and quality of life. After I had finished my study on music and identity, I found that there were many similarities between how music was felt to contribute to a strong, flexible identity and a certain conception of the "quality of life." This meant that *music* could be seen as an important factor in promoting health. Thus, it seemed that this whole journey had come to a temporary conclusion. My initial attempt to formulate a concept of music therapy that gave both music and music therapists an important place within our culture seemed—at least to me—likely to succeed through linking music with identity and health.

Chapter 2

THE INDIVIDUAL AS IMPROVISER: THE CONCEPT OF THE INDIVIDUAL IN MUSIC THERAPY

The field of music therapy is a unique blend of art and science, medicine, and the humanities. It is a treatment profession in which experiences, relationships, reflections, dialogues, and processes are investigated through music communication. Behind the different techniques and methods in music therapy, we find a world of values transferred into various ideals of science. Very different views of such central concepts as *music, science, health, therapy, society,* and *the individual* have led to models of music therapy as different as Creative Music Therapy, Analytical Music Therapy, and Music and Behavioral Therapy. Whatever actions we take as music therapists, we rely on underlying assumptions about the nature of people—that is, on views about questions concerning the role of our biological equipment, language and culture, the nature and role of consciousness, the role of economic and political forces in determining our lives, how we gain knowledge, and so on.

The individual, or *the human being,* is the most basic of these concepts, underlying all the others. We cannot answer the question "What is the individual?" without consequences for our understanding of these other concepts. In this chapter, I will discuss some relationships between the different views on the individual, music, and therapy in several models of music therapy. In addition, I will discuss the question of whether the improvisational approach, because of the unique clinical experiences it generates, may have something to add to our concept of the individual.

THE INDIVIDUAL
AS AN ORGANISM

Theories in general tend toward reduction. Often, in accordance with the positivist ideal of science, we seek to explain complicated things simply—the so-called paradigm of unity. This happens when the individual is reduced to an organism (biology) and music is reduced to acoustics (physics). In music therapy, then, the question of music's influence is reduced to a question of how frequency and amplitude (music) affect our autonomous reactions (emotions).

This way of thinking is rooted in the naturalistic (biological) view of the individual. Originating in the Renaissance, naturalism was popularized in the eighteenth century, mainly because of Isaac Newton and the rise of physics. Some of the main philosophical and epistemological characteristics of the naturalistic philosophy are its materialistic outlook, its evolutionary thought, and its close affiliation with positivism. The naturalistic life view is based on natural science. For instance, we find not only that researchers in biology, physics, and biomedicine have based their research on this line of reasoning but conversely that this research has provided new evidence for the validity of this way of reasoning about the individual.

There are numerous examples of how naturalistic philosophy has influenced the outlook of music therapists. For instance, when illness—including mental illness—is defined, it is grounded in a naturalistic perspective. Humans are regarded as being controlled by biological processes. In medically oriented music therapy, we seek to explain the effects of music by pointing to bodily or physiological changes occurring during the experience of music, or we use neuropsychological theory about music and brain hemispheres to show that music, by detouring through some part of the brain, can reach a part of the mind that is still functioning.

This naturalistic orientation is not a problem in "basic research," in formulating and testing hypotheses about the effects of music. Much important knowledge concerning our bodily reactions to music, especially regarding the crucial role the brain plays in processing our musical behavior and experiences, has come of this research. I am not dismissing naturalistic research or any practice founded on it, whether it be vibroacoustic therapy or anxiolytic applications of music. The problem lies, however, in the connection between this research and a specific scientific philosophy that, because of its marked distinction between so-called analytical and synthetic expressions, wants to exclude any research not based on experience. This theory regards evaluations and logical formal knowledge as subjective and normative and therefore unscientific.

The behavioral part of naturalistic science seems to have had the greatest methodological consequences for clinical music therapy. As Danish science philosopher Hans Siggaard Jensen (1986) pointed out, behavioral music therapy's view of music harmonizes with its naturalistic concept of the individual. Because this research tradition emphasizes measuring the strength and efficiency of music as reinforcement, practitioners avoid discussing research on the nature of music—on why music may be effective as a therapeutic tool. Instead, they assume a concept of music clearly oriented toward need gratification, meaning that music should gratify basic needs for pleasure. Behind this view, we can see that benefit is seen as a central mean value and that pleasure is seen as a central goal value, Jensen argued.

THE INDIVIDUAL
AS A PERSON

Many therapists often stress such nonnaturalistic aspects of the individual as language and thought, capacity for choice and responsibility, and ability to communicate through symbols. Such a humanistic position often both unveils and adds meaning. Music is understood on its own term as an aesthetic phenomenon. The humanistic approach thus makes possible an investigation of connections between musical structure and meaning, or as in therapy, between illness and meaning.

Seen in the naturalistic context, music is defined as a signal of great value in therapy for those seeking to stimulate attention and concentration, to transfer information, or to structure actions or provoke a chain of associations. The humanistic position places more emphasis on music as a symbol, as the creation of a polysemous message through music. In a concept of the individual that emphasizes the significance of language and thought in human change, music may be seen as a vehicle for investigating and making life experiences concrete and manageable, for encouraging hope, and for creating meaning in life.

Humanistic music therapy, then, has to consider basic questions about the individual's subjectivity or her ability to have free choices. In the literature, there is a pronounced tendency to treat the connection between music and experience as a mechanistic one, a stimulus–response connection in which the experiencing person is left out. We might say there is a simplified Pythagorean tradition prevalent in contemporary thought about music therapy, which supposes that a basic force in music effects changes in human behavior. I say "simplified" because in the ancient Pythagorean tradition, there was a strong emphasis on thought and reflection as a component of the cathartic process. An absence of reflection and contemplation of the experience of music threatens to reduce music therapy to pure technology.

This same tendency is evident in the tradition of biomedically oriented music therapy research, both in research on music, emotions, and autonomous reactions and in research on music and brain hemispheres. In both cases, there is no discussion about who is in charge of the perceptual process or about how cognitive and cultural forces are involved in the perceptual process through a centrally positioned "I." In failing to speak about the part of the individual that acts, we reduce the experience of music to a sort of mechanics of the psyche. This is also a danger in psychoanalytic music therapy, whose adherents like to think of music as detouring the ego and intellectual control to directly influence the unconscious.

In the so-called New Age movement, there is a philosophical idealism, a belief in independent forces in music that influence "spiritual forces" in humans. Sometimes we find these ideas in the "newly discovered" Eastern or mystical philosophies, in which music is thought to influence various energy centers in the body, called chakras. What is at work here is the influence of recent physics theories that conceive of materials as "forces." Their "everything is a vibrating mass" philosophy gives music the status of existential massage. The idea of the individual as a self-determined being is left out here, too, as is the necessity of postulating both the "subject" and the "action" as parts of the processes involved.

This "acting subject" is emphasized in improvisation- and dialogue-centered music therapy. When both client and therapist can influence improvisation, we have created a frame that can give the client status as a subject. This can be found, for instance, in the Nordoff-Robbins tradition, in which the client (a child), sometimes without a verbal language, is given the same musical possibilities for action as the adult participant. We could say that the music, because of its nonverbal characteristics, creates a context that makes possible the liberation and installment of an acting "I" by the client. Thus, music does not maintain the structures of power enforced by verbal language that so often in therapy lead to a subject–object relationship. Put another way, music does not support situations in which institutions and authorities prescribe action and ready-made roles tear down initiative and choice.

Even in the humanities, however, there is a tendency toward reduction. Humans are sometimes presented as pure spiritual beings without bodies or cultures. Music thus becomes a universal or spiritual language that influences our minds despite the strictures of history and culture, as in the ancient Pythagorean paradigm. Sometimes, as seen in both old and recent idealistic positions, music is understood as a "natural" personal expression, the meaning of which is extracted from the morphology of music—from the expression's structural significance. When we see music this way, we conceal every trace of cultural interaction that determines the language of music.

One might also object to my proposed emphasis on the "conscious and acting individual" by saying that it too easily disregards 100 years of clinical psychology with its insistence on the more irrational aspects of humankind: the power of body and emotion. It seems truer to music therapy to build theoretical models from a perspective in which experience and action take into consideration both body and emotion. In improvisational as well as receptive music therapy, the question is not just how to process the information inherent in musical codes or just how to read expected meaning. For the clinician, it is just as important to be able to read and deconstruct the meaning growing out of musical interactions. At the same time, we must pay attention to the aesthetic quality of music, the uncontrollable and unpredictable, the experiences that cannot be categorized. Because of this quality, music provides access to the body, to those places within us where experiences originate, and creates a point of departure for the verbal representation of the musical experience. It seems both important and necessary that music therapy preserve music's ability to influence such uninvestigated areas of body and language. Paradoxically, such experiences must be transformed or written into verbal language, which presupposes thought or reflection, unless we want music therapy without verbal language, with the limitations this places on self-understanding and possibilities for action. It is in the rewriting of or telling about nonverbal and sometimes bodily musical experience that music and the musical experience formally become aesthetics. Often in music aesthetics literature, the meaning of music is deduced directly from its structure, thus overlooking the client's own perspective, which is inseparable from the larger context within which the client finds herself. At this "immediate" level, music is not merely a "nonverbal" language; it is a potential polysemous expression.

When music penetrates such uninvestigated areas of body and language and the resulting experiences are translated to or represented by verbal language, possibilities for reaching new verbal or bodily based experiences arise. Such experiences often have to be conceptualized, however, and thus our language not only delimits or conquers our experiences but also makes them explicit. Our inner landscape, the energy-like stream of movement and tension, is given conceptual correlates; in therapy, these are often in the form of defining an image or emotion.

We may read such representations within their cultural context as expressions and negotiations about important themes within a culture. Thus, we may also read the field of musical aesthetics, or the attempt to conceptualize musical experiences (see Chapter 5), as a discourse about power—the power to define concepts and language and therefore the world. Music therapists must have a musical cultural understanding, a deep respect for the individual or idiosyncratic and sometimes subcultural representation of music. If they do not, they reduce themselves to suppliers of a new language or new model through which the client may rewrite her experiences. This in turn deprives the client of the chance to live as deeply as possible through her own preverbal experiences of music.

If the client is allowed to maintain her own cultural position, music may become a catalyst for the rewriting of preverbal experiences. Conceptualized through her language, her emotional life is not only expanded and enriched; as a verbal entity, it is given a form that may be a starting point for reflection and subsequent action. She can then act from an expanded base of experience because she has found new categories through which to treat her inner life. This seems to me a good rationale for a humanistic music therapy, in which the context of a person includes her cultural and social situation.

THE INDIVIDUAL
AS A SOCIAL BEING

In most music therapy models or systems, the larger societal aspects are not sufficiently present. A major problem in music therapy is that the individual is understood only as an organism or as a person while her social background is seen as remote. Often, music therapists stress the adaptation of the individual in relation to the institution or the larger world, not how society can be transformed so it can adapt to people or how music and music therapy can involve participants in meaningful interaction. We need a concept of illness, or rather a concept of health, that stresses preventive care to counteract how modern society itself creates illness.

Another significant problem is that sociophilosophical consequences implicit in various theoretical models of music therapy are seldom discussed. When behavioral music therapists attempt to create a comprehensive archive of all possible reinforcing effects of music, they believe in the myth of an effective, technocratic society. In such a society, all questions about who is going to control whom or about how material or economic structures in an institution or a society may promote symptoms or maladaptive behavior are removed from the discussion. What is held to be the main strength of music in music therapy—namely, its nonverbal character—is used in this one-dimensional view of society to impoverish language and thoughtlessly manipulate basic needs.

Another consequence of taking music therapy out of its broader cultural and social context is that it cannot influence cultural issues concerning the general promotion of health in society. Lately, we have seen attempts in biomedicine to focus on how society and culture may be organized to promote better health.

Looking at the psychology of music underlying many practices and much research in music therapy, we might also conclude that too little emphasis is placed on the relationship between the individual and music being socially or culturally bound. Viewing music as a cultural institution—that is, reading the cultural contexts that create interconnections between music and identity and provide a language for the representation of musical experiences—may help clinicians establish which musical interactions are basic to therapeutic intervention. Acting musically in accordance with the client's repertoire of musical codes means not only a better foundation for musical dialogues but also a basic respect for the musical identity of the client, her "musical human rights," and ultimately her human dignity (Stefani, 1989).

This attempt to explain how our musical socialization, or our concept of the individual, is determined by society's structure and economic conditions may also have its weaknesses. This line of reasoning may lead to what is called "mechanical materialism"—that is, a concept of the individual in which she is stripped of her position as client and from which there is no subjectivity of body, emotion, or language.

AN ECOLOGICAL APPROACH

Instead of reducing our concepts of music and the individual to one dimension of our existence, it seems more reasonable to emphasize music therapy's interdisciplinary nature. We need a concept of the individual in which biological, psychological, and sociological factors are considered necessary for an understanding of the client's relationship with music and how this relationship can be used in therapeutic strategy.

This concept entails a shift, however, from a paradigm of unity to one of complexity, one of holism. To me, looking holistically at music therapy implies that organismic, personal, and social aspects of the individual are all taken into consideration. This approach seems to fit well with system theory, which focuses on ecological aspects of the individual and her relationship with nature. Carolyn Kenny brought system theory to music therapy. In her book *The Field of Play* (1989), she outlined a broad perspective on the many interacting disciplines in music therapy. In general, system theory implies a more ecological outlook on humans and nature; that is, it stresses their interdependency.

In some of the last chapters in this book, we will discuss how communication theory may be applied in music therapy. Such concepts as symmetrical and complementary interaction, punctuation, and a circular model of cause and effect are examples of this way of thinking. Furthermore, I think that a system approach to music therapy may help us plan our music therapy interventions so that behavior changes are maintained through changes in the whole system surrounding the client. For example, music therapy interventions could be directed toward parents and the ways they and their children communicate, rather than focusing only on the child. Training parents or staff to become better communicators with music could ensure that improvement in clients' behavior would be sustained after therapeutic intervention. Other examples of a system-oriented approach would be to bring music therapy activities into the community and to build social networks through music groups.

THE INDIVIDUAL
AS IMPROVISER

One main question remains to be asked: How can experiences from music therapy teach us something about the individual and how does this knowledge fit into our concept of the individual?

Later, I will show how improvisation can be regarded as basic to social interaction and how, through music, we can learn to communicate about communication. In Chapter 10, I will argue how the transitional nature of music can enhance play and fantasy, provide new means for exploring the client's inner life, and offer a mode for investigating life's possibilities. Improvisation thus makes possible the "psychological fantasy" we need to translate tacit experiences into verbal concepts. Put another way, a kind of sociological or anthropological fantasy may help us see what kind of negotiations are going on between the client and her cultural system.

In a world in which the formerly highly valued "acting subject" has become a sort of "instrumental reason" that has made human beings outsiders and rulers of nature and the environment, we must work toward a concept of humankind in which ecological aspects—humankind's coexistence with its environment—is put into focus. It is possible that sometimes in the near future, we might need an "improvising individual" as a basis for the acting individual, an individual who can live in a process in which inner stability and safety, as both presuppositions and results of the ability to improvise, enable psychic flexibility. This would be someone who not only can readjust herself to a changeable world but whose verbal descriptions of reality are extensively based on bodily reactions, their psychic rewriting, and an understanding of the cultural processes and their interaction with her society's political and economical structures. If music therapy understands itself as a part of a cultural movement and not only as a treatment profession, it may contribute significantly to such a concept of the individual.

Perhaps improvisation as a way of making music together may be a good metaphor for our understanding of the individual. In improvisation, we often start from scratch, from some preliminary ideas we want to follow. Although we may have some broader ideas of where we want to go, we can never be sure of either the route to follow or the final goal. The whole process involves other people. The music we make is influenced by others in a circular manner, as are the plans for life we make. In the process, we may find a new tempo, transpose, take risks, and meet crises involving a possible breakdown in the improvisation—much in the same way as in life. There are new musical expectations to be set up, disappointments, fulfillment, and temporary closure. We sometimes go along with others' melodies, although we may change them, transpose them, or invent our own. Always in a process full of immediacy and spontaneity, we may participate fully with others. Not only the music grooves; sometimes our contact with others does, too. Through the process of improvisation, we may come up with a product in a certain style, creating our own piece of musical identity, much in the same sense that personal identity is improvised and narrated.

Chapter 3

MUSIC AND IDENTITY

All of us have had the feeling sometimes that there is a connection between the music we prefer to listen to and the people we are—perhaps not too literally, but metaphorically. We like to refer to our collections of tapes or CDs or the music we prefer to listen to as "my music" (Crafts et al., 1993). Sometimes we may also have the feeling that music reaches deep into or mirrors our personalities—our "true selves," as some like to call it. We certainly are offended if someone tells us we have bad taste in music. We engage in the game of sorting other people into broad sociological categories on the basis of their musical taste, often supported by observations about the ways they dress, move, and talk. We act as if such pigeonholing were possible: "Tell me what kind of music you like and I'll tell you who you are."

My theories grew out of the vague intuition that there might be some connection between music and the way we look at and present ourselves. After struggling with this idea for what turned out to be more than 15 years, I would have to state the hypothesis differently today. Listening to, performing, and talking about music is not as much a reflection of identity as a way of *performing* our sense of ourselves, our identities. This makes a difference in the way we perceive how a sense of identity is constituted.

Instead of engaging in speculations, I set out to design a study. From Kenneth Bruscia at the 1982 symposium in New York, Music in the Life of Man, I got the idea of asking my music therapy students to write their musical autobiographies. In the context of my teaching systematic musicology in the music therapy training courses in Oslo and Sandane, I found this approach to be a valuable teaching and learning technique. It allowed students to apply academic knowledge to their lives; the emphasis was on doing and learning instead of passively receiving ideas. Opportunities for dialogue and group work were rich, and the teaching material became highly meaningful.

All 20 students in the first group were asked to present me with a cassette tape of 10 to 15 pieces of music they felt were significant in their lives. On the basis of this tape, all students were interviewed for about 1 hour. All interviews were recorded and later transcribed and analyzed. An additional 40 students were asked to give me, together with a tape, a 10-page typed commentary on the music selected. These interviews and autobiographies, or "musical memory work," as I later preferred to call them, were analyzed along the guidelines of the Strauss-Corbin version of grounded theory (1990).

The task of the analysis has been to make explicit the main theme of this study, which is "music and identity," through constructing some core categories from the material. Furthermore, I sought to give these categories a richer description by identifying relevant subcategories or dimensions in each category.

The focus of the analysis transcripts and autobiographical statements was the musical experiences and the events that contextualized them. I did not analyze the song texts or the musical structure of the songs presented on the tapes, nor did I analyze, except in my own musical autobiography, any person in depth in the form of a case study. Through close reading of the reports, I was looking for statements about the experiences of music that could be related to any category of identity. At the same time, I did extensive reading of the literature on identity, mainly within sociological and cultural studies, psychology, and anthropology. Throughout the years, I tried out many sets of categories based on my intuition, reading, and discussions with colleagues. Gradually, I came up with a set of four categories that I felt covered all aspects of music and identity. The validity of the categories has been supported in recent years by further collections of data and feedback from people reading my publications on music and identity. Because this chapter is only a short version of my findings and does not contain any of the original stories included in the material, I am aware that it may be difficult for readers to confirm my categories. I have, however, published my complete findings in a book (Ruud, 1997a) that includes a large number of the stories, as well as my own musical autobiography. (I hope there will be an English translation of this study in the future.)

These categories are presented more thoroughly later in this chapter, but generally, they were as follows: music and personal space, musical and social space, the space of time and place, and transpersonal space. Among the almost 1,000 musical experiences or short narratives about musical incidences that I have analyzed, all were related to one or often more of these categories. In this chapter, however, I will concentrate on the theoretical aspects of the study.

There are many methodological aspects to be discussed in relation to such a study (Ruud, 1995a). A few points should be mentioned here. First, there is a lack of relevant research studies in the literature on the psychology of music. Swedish music psychologist Alf Gabrielsson and his associates, however, have conducted rather extensive interviews with more than 800 people regarding "strong musical experiences." Gabrielsson has so far published only some aspects of his material (Gabrielsson and Lindström, 1994, 1995; see also Stefani, 1996). Gabrielsson refers to a study conducted by Panzerella, who gathered descriptions of peak experiences in relation to art from 103 people (see Jørgensen, 1989). In contrast to Gabrielsson and Panzerella, however, I decided early on not to focus only on "deep," "peak," or strong musical experiences. Rather, I instructed the participants in the study, perhaps rather vaguely, to gather stories, from their whole lives, of musical experiences that they remembered for some reason. Drawing on theories from a broader theoretical perspective—that is, from cultural studies, sociology, and anthropology of music, as well as from clinical music therapy and research—I was interested in the more tacit themes of life bound to the context of listening situations as revealed through the verbal or written reports given to me.

Methodologically, we may understand how this "musical map" is linked to the construction of identity by studying the local discourses that take place around musical practice. This sometimes necessitates the use of detailed ethnographic studies. As anthropologist Steven Feld (1984) has argued, music listening is a thoroughly social process guided by a set of interpretative moves. When we listen to a piece of music, we locate it in our cultural

soundscape. Through categorical interpretative moves, we may
relate the music we listen to with a particular genre. At the same
instant, we make various associational moves when we relate or
analogize the musical item to particular visual, musical, or verbal
imagery. To this process we may add both reflective moves, relating the music to some personal and social conditions, and evaluative moves, instantly placing the piece on some scale of value. It is
through externalizing this process of interpretation, through
interviews, or when we observe a musical practice that we gain
access to the maps or cognitive strategies used by the people in
question. It is wise to remember that we cannot grasp the meaning of value judgments of music unless we participate in a situation in which language is being used, a corollary to the view, held
by Ludwig Wittgenstein and his followers, that language gains
meaning through use.

Gabrielsson and Lindström (1995) also made an interesting
statement about the problem of the distance in time between the
experience and the moment of representing it. I am not concerned, however, about the truth value or the exactness of how an
experience is felt. I am interested instead in the possible distortion of memory as a part of the process of constructing meaningful
memories as raw material in the identity-building process. The
possible distortion is evidence of the person's actively constructing
her life into a coherent and meaningful narrative that she experiences as personal identity. Among other important theoretical and
methodological influences are the feminist studies on "memory
work" by Haug et al. (1983), recent studies in the field of music
anthropology and cultural studies by Keil and Feld (1994), and
discourse-oriented and narrative approaches, represented by
Freeman (1993) and Widdershoven (1993).

THE CONCEPT OF
IDENTITY

There is no general agreement in the literature about how
to define *identity*. In one sense, *identity* refers to an individual's
particular combination of personal characteristics, such as name, age,
gender, profession, and so on. This more public aspect of identity con-

trasts with the inner, experiential side of self-awareness. In social and personality psychology, *identity* is sometimes used to describe dimensions within the personality, or traits that distinguish people. In a more subjective, phenomenological sense, we may speak about a "feeling" or "awareness" of identity. In this sense, *identity* then refers to a person's consciousness about "being the same," the experience of continuity, and about being unique from others.

There is a range of concepts used to describe this feeling of individual distinction. Apart from the concept of identity itself, we can find in the literature such categories as *person, self, ego, individual, self-concept,* and *ego ideal.* Of these, the concept of self seems most important in this interdisciplinary context. Although the concept of self may be differently conceived in various theoretical traditions, there seems to be some general common understanding that *self* refers to our own person, to what I feel and think about myself.

There are different opinions, however, about the status of this self within the larger morphology of the person. In psychoanalytic theory, the self is regarded as a subjective or mental content, a product of the ego. The self is regarded as partly unconscious, like many feelings, fantasies, or thoughts. In the humanistic tradition in psychology, *self* may be used in a more ontological way, to refer to some kind of personal essence, an "inner core," "the very me." Within this tradition, one may also speak about "the true self," and the concept of *self-realization* suggests some kind of preexisting potential core to be actualized within a personal growth process.

Self is used in a more functional way among authors who emphasize the self as "agent"—that is, the acting or motivational aspect of the self-construct. The self is conceived as a unifying principle that integrates the individual's activities, much in the same sense as the neopsychoanalytic concept of *ego.*

Although it is sometimes difficult to distinguish the discourse about self from the terms *self-concept, self-image,* or *the perceived self,* the term *self-concept* seems to imply a more cognitive processing than does *the perceived self,* which may, I think, also refer to more general perceptions of the body. The concept *self-esteem,* on the other hand, refers to the evaluative aspect of the self-concept.

The sense of identity is first of all anchored in a presupposed sense of a self. This sense of self or individuality is in part my sense of experiencing the world from a particular location in space, the location of my body (Harré and Gillett, 1994, p. 107). Identity is rooted in the particular discourse the individual performs when her consciousness is monitoring her own activities, memories, and fantasies. In selecting from the possible life circumstances and memories and through projecting these toward the future, the individual narrates a concept of the self to herself as a negotiated identity. Working from a narrative model, we may say that the individual's identity results from a particular discourse the consciousness has engaged in, the special way of framing or contextualizing her own life experiences. In this construction, we can recognize the metaphoric tools used to structure and give meaning to the story of identity.

The theoretical model of such a narrated identity, as it is explicated within different theoretical traditions, may again be regarded as an academic discourse, leading to the definition of *identity* as an "academic metaphor for self in context" (Fitzgerald, 1993, p. 3). This may lead us to question which academic tradition or theoretical framework is to take part in this discourse. As we have seen, psychology emphasizes ontological or relational aspects of identity as well as more basic bodily sensations or awareness. Extending this discourse to include transpersonal psychologists, we may include transcendental experiences, or aspects of meaning and values within our construction of ourselves. (Thanks to Carolyn Kenny for drawing my attention to this body of literature and field of study and for discussions leading to the formation of the category of *transpersonal space*. Also, thanks to Barbara Zanchi and La Music Interna [Bologna] for introducing me to the works of Assagioli, which helped me confirm this category.) Anthropology and sociology bring a larger cultural and historical context into focus because they emphasize the aspects of time and space in the construction of identity. Sociologists also stress current social conditions for the construction of identity and draw our attention to how our embeddedness within different social and cultural fields may condition our sense of belongingness to a certain class, ethnic group, or gender.

Music cannot mechanically depict identities, social formations, ideologies, or private value systems, but it may encode such dimensions. It is my interpretative activity, often as a participant in a broader interpretative community, that brings forth such meaning, however. Music may be thought of as an object we act toward in order to make obvious our values and our actual position in culture (see Ruud, 1996a). It is all the talk about music that gives it its meaning; it is the discourses about "authenticity," taste, style, genre, and "quality" that together give music its cultural content.

This conglomerate of ideas and conceptions of identity provides us, as music therapists, with a rich base on which to build our categories of music and identity. Music, because it is ever present in our daily lives, frames and anchors many of the situations used as a raw material in the process of identity-building. In light of the emotional quality of musical experiences, it seems to me that these feeling-filled memories may serve an important role because they highlight and position people's life events significantly. For the field of music therapy, as an applied part of systematic musicology, a more specific grasp of how music helps to construe a sense of identity is an important tool for perceiving and understanding clinical events.

We may say that what characterizes identity in our (post)modern culture is, in large part, reflexivity (Giddens, 1991). Identity no longer comes to us ready-made, because identity is a process, something never fulfilled. Identity is constructed at the same time we make the grid or model for whom we want to be and where we want to belong. In this grid or matrix, our private self and bodily sensibilities, a sense of history and of local and global attachment, social relations, and the experience of personal agency seem to be important parameters.

To study identity implies to look for "the means a person employs for the discursive presentation of oneself as a self, a unique person" (Harré and Gillett, 1994, p. 103). This sense of one's personal individuality means to have "a place or places in various manifolds, that is, systems of locations" (Harré and Gillett, 1994, p. 103). It is a sense of being quadrupally located, Harré and Gillett elaborated: a sense of location in space, literally; a sense of existing at a moment in an unfolding of time—that is, of one's life as a trajectory or path through time; a sense of one's responsibility as an agent located in a network of mutual obligations and commitments to other people; and a social place, a location in a manifold of people ordered by status, age, reputation, and the like.

IDENTITY, EMOTION, AND
BODY AWARENESS:
PERSONAL SPACE

There seems to be basic agreement in the literature about the social nature of the self, an agreement traceable back to Erikson, who wrote, "The conscious feeling of having a personal identity is based on two simultaneous observations: the perception of the self sameness and continuity of one's existence in time and space and the perception of the fact that others recognize one's sameness and continuity" (Erikson, 1968, p. 50).

Although we may acknowledge that the feeling of a self is present from early life onward, as in Daniel Stern's concept of a "core self" based on the infant's early recognition of continuity and of feelings and on the ability to create a structure and transfer meanings (Stern, 1991; Wrangsjö, 1994), the presence of other people seems crucial to making the child conscious of her own perceptions. Other people are necessary for us to be visible to ourselves. This may lead to an exploration of how our relationships to other people throughout life plays an important part in the construction of our identity. This aspect of interaction theory has also lately been explored by music therapists, who find many similarities between this recent understanding of child development and the improvisational form of music therapy, as I will discuss later (see also Johns, 1993; Rolvsjord, 1996).

What the French philosopher Gabriel Marcel calls "being with" appears to be a necessary condition for the formation of an identity. As psychologist Ruthellen Josselson writes:

> In order to tell the story of identity fully, we would have to speak in stereo, one speaker voicing the themes of doing and self, the other carrying the counterpoint of connection.

Although identity is in part distinct, differentiated self-hood, it is also an integration of relational contexts that profoundly shape, bound, and limit but also create opportunities for the emergent identity (Josselson, 1994, p. 89).

This view contrasts with much theorizing about identity in terms of individuality, separateness, actions, self-confirmation, mastery, values, and abstract commitment. These stories might be gender-biased, although there is no sense in thinking that the relational aspect of identity-building is less important for men than for women in our society. This may be true for adolescents as well, who are often regarded as going through a period of separation-individuation, but they are not becoming "lone selves," Josselson argues:

Rather, they are editing and modifying, enriching and extending their connections to others, becoming more fully themselves in relation. Individuation is reinvested in revised relatedness, and in these commitments lies the integration of identity (Josselson, 1994, p. 83).

When people talk or write about their first musical memories, we often hear stories about parents or grandparents who sang lullabies or played songs. These songs framed or anchored the person in her early memories of "being held" and supported within a trustworthy relationship. The song often creates strong memories of the person behind the song, thus recalling the person as a symbol of trust and faith in life, or letting the song symbolically represent this feeling. Frequently, the song is recalled during frightening situations later in life, helping the person to overcome a difficult task. The feelings of warmth and harmony brought forth by the song are often reenacted through the song's performance.

An important part of this music-making is that the child is often "seen" by the adult. The musical situation creates a privileged position: the child occupies the adult's full attention, what psychoanalyst Heinz Kohut called "the gleam in the eye" of the other, something that makes the child accept herself and feel at home in herself.

There is a connection between feelings and a sense of self. Feelings may be regarded as a system of information carrying sensations of how the person feels at home in the world, how the body adapts to the situation. Awareness of feelings and bodily sensations may thus be said to be an important part of self-awareness (Monsen, 1991). This awareness may be divided into ability for attention and expression. Emotional attention is demonstrated through the many vivid reports of memories of early musical experiences, in which dramatic emotions often are displayed and narrated. In the Norwegian song tradition, we have an old genre called *skillingsviser,* or pennytunes, which in earlier times were often composed and used to bring news and to entertain. Among these songs are dramatized narratives about people who suffer or are treated unfairly and stories about sick children and loved ones who die. Children often prefer these songs but may report the terror the songs created, the dark emotions that made them cry and suffer. In spite of this, I found in my material that these children still wanted to listen to the songs over and over again. This was often accompanied by a shared experience with an adult who helped the child to discover and comprehend the emotion felt. Thus, it could seem that these songs became some sort of training in emotional tolerance, in the ability to contain and sustain emotion.

I found that at the same time, these emotional exercises could become an arena for conceptual description and clarification of emotions, thus helping the child express different emotions to the world. Of course, music in itself also becomes part of the repertoire of ways of responding to the world. Children learn how to select music for listening that matches their moods and emotions. This way of reasoning about emotional awareness is demonstrated in stories about bodily reactions to music. Later in adolescence, these bodily reactions may be aesthetically enjoyed for their own value, often reported in stories about the joy of turning music on very loud—sometimes reported as a kind of "audiological piercing."

Among the metaphors chosen to represent some of the more personal reactions to music, I found in the musical autobiographies such concepts as "private space," "inner core," and "private room." To listen to music or play an instrument appears to lead to an awareness of a space within oneself that is totally distinct and not accessible to other people. Sometimes this is called the "true self," which may be dramatically met by a sudden mood in the music or by a voice or an artist. Thus, unfamiliar music was compared to "unknown rooms" or undiscovered parts of the self, as though the self were topographically divided in space. Talking to some of the autobiographers who also defined themselves as performers, I learned how a special genre was experienced as "too narrow" to represent their own self-conceptualization. To express the "true self," they sought other genres or made hybrid constellations of music, mixing, for instance, jazz and folk music. In this picture, a "false self" sometimes appeared, as in the stories told about being forced to practice, perform, or play an instrument that was not felt as the autobiographers' own chosen activity.

There were many stories that reflected feelings of mastery and achievement. Music provides opportunities to feel appreciated by the family and the larger community. Happy instances of immediate reward, recognition, and praise feed the self-esteem, the evaluating aspects of the self. These positive experiences empower the person and lay the ground for agency, achievement, and mastery, key concepts in the formation of identity.

MUSIC AND SOCIAL SPACE

The recognition of the interpersonal aspects of identity leads to a greater awareness of the role of the larger cultural context wherein identity takes form. In contrast to the feeling of rootlessness, where the person misses the sense of embeddedness, we know how a person can feel embedded in her context. Psychologist Erik H. Erikson (1968, p. 22) underlined how our identity not only concerned the "core" in the individual but also had to be sought in our communality with others.

This sense of being part of a larger social and cultural group, in a specific historical time and situated in a particular place, is particularly emphasized by anthropologists when they set out to study "the others." Being a part of a social group also positions the individual in a particular way within a culture, as a member of a social class, within a particular ethnic group, or within a gender reality. In our own field, we could say we are using music to create boundaries between ourselves and others and to communicate where we belong within a larger social landscape. We may also let our choice in music symbolize our value attachment with others.

Many of the stories I gathered also deal with an emerging experience of individuality, the roots of which might have been formed in early childhood. Although most children, at least as far as their early school years, seem to share the musical values of their parents, I found that some children grew up with parents who outspokenly disliked each other's music, making the child aware of the concept of musical taste at a young age. When a child meets the outside world, she compared her own taste with those of the social and cultural groups in the community, thus giving her a sense of social space. Music may come to symbolize triviality or adventure or may fuel the search for individuality.

When the young child meets the social world through different taste cultures, she may also gain important social knowledge—about how the social world is perceived from different social positions—through partaking in discourse about music. In this sense, to be engaged in music is to learn basic social competencies or communicative skills (Frønes, 1994).

Children's first conscious steps away from their family or community values are often signaled through musical taste. Although most people keep their bonds with their parents intact, they may indicate their emotional separation from their parents— opposition, rebellion, protest, and so on—through the music they choose. Through processes of identification, adolescents may use idols from the music world to try out different identities, which they then present to others to get reactions in a sort of "data collection." The music world thus becomes a kind of "re-dressing room" for identity work.

Sometimes I read music autobiographies whose authors had a sense of living in a model of reality that they felt was not in accordance with its description by parents or authorities (Berkaak, 1993). Such a dilemma sometimes leads to a search for a more authentic way of being. This search for authenticity is a peculiarly Western form of identity construction that finds its origins in eighteenth-century philosophy (see Taylor, 1995). I read many reports about how a person suddenly heard music or saw an artist perform whose work seemed a more "true" representation of life, or about how music sometimes matched a mood or inner feeling that helped the person define a new life direction. Sometimes this experience of authenticity in music is described in such terms as "longing/finding" or "searching/discovering," as if the person has discovered something that was already there but only just then became apparent.

The construction of gender is, of course, important here. Often, girls report finding an artist with a voice that represents their own self-image or one who helps them feel strong and independent. Thus, music empowers the young or helps them identify with an adequately felt sense of gender.

Although musical taste may be used to delimit, mark, or communicate social and cultural values, we cannot say that music or musical taste just mirrors social class, economic stratum, or education level. There is research, however, that shows that it is possible within a cultural system to perform a sort of sociological typification on the basis of musical taste (Lewis, 1995). French cultural sociologist Pierre Bourdieu has shown that economic and cultural capital are often connected and that musical taste is embodied in a sort of "habitus" that transforms our cultural consumption into a kind of mark of identity. Recent work in the anthropology of music, though, is more concerned with music as a means of producing and transforming social reality. Music not only depicts a social position but also transforms social space and boundaries (Stokes, 1994). As Simon Frith, scholar of popular music, stated, "Making music isn't a way of expressing ideas; it is a way of living them" (Frith, 1996, p. 11).

THE SPACE OF
TIME AND PLACE

Identity is particularly connected with where I come from, the geographical space I feel attached to. It also concerns the time I have lived through and feel connected to. When I experience music, it will always be at a certain time, in a certain space. Time and place are intimately related through the musical experience.

Musical experiences may be regarded as markers of important life events. Some events may be permanently fixed in memory because they mark the transition from one phase of life to another. They thus construct a sense of my personal calendar and give me a basis from which to compare my sense of lived time with the public sense of time. Through my memory work, I construct coherence and continuity in my life, regarding my life as a continuous trajectory with a beginning, a present, and an ending (see Giddens, 1991; Harré and Gillett, 1994).

If I look at my own experiences, I can sometimes refer to personal experiences of music, such as concerts, that not only were significant events in my life but also later became important historical public events. Thus, I remember the concerts given by Charlie Mingus and John Coltrane in Oslo in the early 1960s as important biographical events, as a part of my "organic history." These embodied experiences, which form an important part of my own sense of history, may be correlated with the written record in history books. In this sense, my sense of history gains a historical dimension that is synchronized with the social and public ways of writing history (see Berkaak, 1993, p. 102).

Music also helps to ritualize time into "cyclic time"—time that repeats itself. Radio and television punctuate the week into discrete episodes and thus create the impression of time as something that is divided into parts and moves ahead. Certain television programs become synonymous with a certain day, and some people do not really feel it is Christmas before they have heard a certain melody on the radio.

When I perform the story of who I am, the place I come from seems especially important. Music is used to symbolize my nationality, especially when I am abroad. Not only my nation's anthem but every tune that reminds me of my nationality seems to bring out nationalism. In contemporary global society, however, we do not just come from a certain country or are not just international; instead, we are increasingly attached to both regional and local geography and culture. In Norway, several regional musical movements have brought new pride in local identity. Such music brings forth the typical regional feelings of belonging through connotations of local nature and ways of life. Some of the autobiographers in my study told stories about how they had taped their own regional music to use in comforting themselves when their longing for home became too strong.

In this respect, folk music becomes especially important. Although young people often do not recognize their local folk music, they reported that they were often impressed with other people's folk music when they were abroad. This sometimes led to a revitalization of their own interest in local traditions. This interest in music and place seemed to be linked to the construction and maintenance of ethnicity.

TRANSPERSONAL SPACE

As I remarked earlier, when identity is defined as an academic metaphor for self in context, we must pay attention to who defines the academic tradition on which to model our understanding of the context. If we include transpersonal psychologists in this academic discourse, we will also have to look at how identity includes experiences of meaning—that is, at how our life may be perceived as part of some larger order, a transcendental space, or a religious dimension.

Sometimes our music experiences make us feel something indefinite and indescribable, something beyond the limits of language. This experience, which in the field of aesthetics is described as "the sublime," may be ascribed to the feeling of belonging to a greater reality, to be in touch with something greater than our everyday world. This experience is often described in terms of being "taken away," moving "out" of ourselves, being outside time and place. Often, people experience strong bodily reactions, as if their bodies and minds were full of energy and power (Gabrielsson and Lindström, 1994; Ruud, 1997a; Stefani, 1996). These strong experiences may sometimes be perceived as having a therapeutic quality or effect (Gabrielsson and Lindström, 1995).

Transpersonal psychologists have focused on experiences like these, and several from tradition of psychosynthesis have studied them (Assagioli, 1988). More familiar, perhaps, is Maslow's concept of "peak experiences," or "acute experiences of identity":

> Since my feeling is that most people in peak-experiences are
> *most* their identities, closest to their real selves, most idiosyn-
> cratic, it would seem that this is an especially important
> source of clean and uncontaminated data (Maslow, 1968, p.
> 103).

In other words, we could say that music experiences like these
contribute to an altered state of consciousness (Bonny and Savary,
1973), an experience sometimes similar to the trance state found
in transitional rituals. I describe in Chapter 8 how in the liminal
phase of these rituals (see also Ruud, 1992a; Turner, 1974), the
person reports finding herself in a space in which known references disappear, symbols seem to lose their conventional significance, and time and space dissolve. In this state, she may
experience new meaning being added to her identity. When people
tried to transcribe this experience into language, they report the
recognition of something divine, being a part of something larger
than life," or being part of a greater order and continuity. This
phenomenon adds an existential dimension to our identity that
gives us the feeling that we are anchored in a reality outside ourselves. Our identity becomes rooted in a transpersonal space.

IMPROVISATION:
A METAPHOR FOR IDENTITY

Music plays an important role in the construction of identity
within the mediascape that surrounds us from birth to death.
Music can serve as raw material for building values and life ori-
entations, as a way to anchor important relationships to other
people, as a way of framing our situatedness in a certain time and
space, and as a way to position ourselves within our culture and
thus make explicit our ethnicity, gender, and class. It also provides important "peak" or transcendental experiences that may
strengthen the formation of identity in the sense that we feel
meaning, purpose, and significance in our life.

The issue of identity plays an increasingly important role in
our effort to understand humankind in the late modern area. As
an interdisciplinary construct, the concept of identity brings

together theories and knowledge from psychology, the humanities, anthropology, and sociology to map some of the conditions for everyday conduct in a complex society.

The issue of music and identity is important for the field of music therapy in several ways. First, we should be aware of our own musical identity. Knowing the role of music in some of our significant life experiences may increase our sensitivity to our own cultural background and personal history, which extends to our body and early interpersonal relationships and makes us aware of deeper transcendental experiences. The knowledge of how music helps construct an individual's self-concept may help us choose the right music for our clients—the proper music to empower people within their own cultural context. Because significant people and situations are often embedded in musical experiences, using music to create memories about significant events may heighten the potential for therapeutic work in the music therapy session. I argue that because music is related to identity-building, it may contribute to the quality of life. Thus, we can argue that music is related to broader issues of health in society.

As David Aldridge has suggested, music may be a better metaphor for identity than the "organismic" or "machine" metaphors often found in the literature (Aldridge, 1996). We may regard our lives as composed of the many themes and values that we live by, as counterpoints in a complex composition. Through our idiosyncratic performance of our life practice and competencies, we form a personal identity in the same way composers construct their music or performers play music (Ruud, 1997a). As I suggested in Chapter 2, perhaps we improvise rather than compose our lives. Our lives are not lived according to a preset plan, so if we compose while being in the process, improvisation may be a better metaphor.

Chapter 4

MUSIC, HEALTH, AND
QUALITY OF LIFE

The history of music therapy reveals that new findings in dominant philosophical or scientific thought have often been assimilated as new rationales for the use of music in treating disease and in maintaining health. The way in which we think about health and quality of life has implications for how music therapy is defined. As I will attempt to show, it may also be that music therapy has much to offer in regard to quality of life.

Since its beginnings in the 1950s, the field of music therapy has grown from just a few individual pioneers to a large social formation of professionals with their own values and ideologies about music and health. The question is how music therapy, as a social formation, may influence general thinking about such issues in today's society. When health authorities talk about the role of cultural activity in promoting mental health in society, they do not always recognize that music therapists and other art therapists pioneered this way of thinking. The purpose of this chapter, then, is to devise a formal concept of a musical hygienics for clinicians to take with them into general society. In this hygienics, music serves an important role in promoting quality of life because it strengthens our emotional awareness, installs a sense of agency, fosters belongingness, and provides meaning and coherence in life.

TWO HISTORICAL TRENDS

From the point of view of the sociology of knowledge, as I remarked in the introduction, it is understandable that music therapy, when first established as an academic discipline in the United States in the 1950s, had to depart from all kinds of metaphysical or idealistic types of theory to gain respect in the prevailing scientific community. In the creation of the science and the profession of music therapy, however, the question of the general role and value of music in everyday life was somewhat neglected. The concept of music as therapy won much scientific credibility but lost its historically important role as a field of knowledge that uses music as an important source of information about how to live in and relate to the world.

This more general approach to the role of music in relation to health and illness can be illustrated with a few examples from the history of music therapy. Two prevailing concepts run through the Western history of music therapy from ancient Greece up to the nineteenth century. One concept has to do with the ways music relates to different concepts of illness—for instance, the ancient theory of the four humors. The other concept is more concerned with how music can be seen within a larger hygienics frame—that is, how music can contribute to "the good life." An illustration of this last concept is how music in ancient Greece was considered to be among those activities which could restore peace and harmony. Together, the hygienics approach and the theory of humoral pathology, in combination with the ancient music aesthetics theory of "ethos," became a strong base for the application of music in medicine throughout the centuries. According to German historian Werner Friedrich Kümmel (1977, p. 20), this tradition lasted until the early nineteenth century.

When we look at how music is related to different concepts of illness, one of the first ideas we find in the Western history of music therapy is a belief in music as a general strengthener of the mind, in its general prophylactic power. This medical model shows up among the so-called prescientific explanations, in which illness was thought to be caused by a worm or an animal entering the body, such as the chimera, a fantasy animal with the head of a lion, the body of a goat, and the tail of a snake. This idea prevailed in ancient Greece in the medical center of Epidauros (sixth century B.C.); both cultural and medical activities were built on such beliefs (Papadakis, 1971, p. 9). The ultimate goal of treatment was to strengthen the mind so that the fantasy animal could not enter. (It is of note that this view has the same structure as our contemporary bacteriological theory.)

Other ancient theories regarded illness as disharmony, either spiritual, as in the lack of harmony in the Pythagorean system, or inner, between the body humors (humoral pathology). Music was thought to restore harmony, either because it reflected the numbers of the macrocosmos (according to the Pythagorean or "allopathic" effect) or because it cleansed the body through cathartic activity (according to Aristotle's "isopathic" effect).

Later in history, these theories were reworked to align with existing medical and philosophical beliefs. In the fifteenth century, Neoplatonic philosopher Marsilio Ficino wrote that cultural workers especially needed music, pleasant surroundings, and a glass of wine to counteract the accumulation of black gall that could result from hard study.

In the seventeenth century, the mechanistic philosophy of René Descartes, combined with the affect theory of the music aesthetic of the Baroque period, laid the basis for a theory of music (therapy) that stressed that the intervals of music could expand or contract the *spiritus animale* of the body and therefore directly influence state of mind. Then, a century later, the "vitalist" concept in medicine held that illness did not have any material basis but was to be seen as a distraction of the pure spirit. Music was thus justified in therapy because of its ability to reach these pre-intellectual spheres of the mind.

In the nineteenth century, however, music seemed to lose its cultural role as a general therapeutic force. This was due in part to the weakening of the concept of hygienics in medicine and in part to the growth of the positivist philosophy of science, with its emphasis on the experimental method or natural science-based procedures.

CONCEPTS OF HEALTH
AND QUALITY OF LIFE

When I first attempted to define music therapy, I was concerned that I not create a definition placing the client in a "sick" role. In traditional medical thinking, therapy is connected to some kind of disease or illness, often related, in Western medicine, to our biology. In addition, there is also a tendency in our culture to regard disease as something that strikes the individual independent of society and culture. We could thus say that our medicine is oriented toward illness and based on a biological and individualistic concept of disease. (I discriminate between the two terms *disease* and *illness* in the sense that *disease* is understood as a pathological process, whereas *illness* is "a feeling, an experience of unhealth which is entirely personal, interior to the person or the patient. Sometimes illness exists where no disease can be found" [Nordenfelt, 1991a, p. 92].) Furthermore, this way of looking at illness is conceived within a natural-science way of thinking, in accordance with the above-mentioned concept of illness from ancient Greece: "something" that gets into the body. Today, though, that something is no longer a fantasy animal, but a virus or bacteria.

Because music therapists work with a broad range of life problems and handicaps, this way of thinking about therapy and illness is not adequate, of course, in many instances. Sometimes we work with clients whose problems may be deeply interwoven with the material and economic structure of society, or whose problems are shaped more by their own attitudes and reflections, as well as by the attitudes of others, rather than by their individual or objective biological constitution.

This is why I came up with the idea of defining music therapy as an effort to "increase the possibilities for action." To increase a person's possibilities for action would mean not only to empower her but also to alleviate—through changing the context of music therapy—some of the material or psychological forces that keep her in a handicapped role. I was aware, however, that this definition was too broad to give a precise picture of what a music therapist can do. I therefore find much sense in other more detailed attempts to describe our profession. An example is the most recent definition offered by the World Federation of Music Therapy: "Music therapy is the use of music and/or its musical elements (sound, rhythm, melody, and harmony) by a music therapist, and client or group, in a process designed to facilitate and promote communication, relationship, learning, mobilization, expression, and organization (physical, emotional, mental, social, and cognitive) in order to develop potentials and develop or restore functions of the individual so that he or she can achieve better intra- and/or interpersonal integration and, consequently, a better quality of life" (Lia Rejane Barcellos, personal communication, May 31, 1996).

One aspect of this definition regards music therapy as a way to move toward a better quality of life. There is a tendency to equate "quality of life" with "health." First, I will address the latter concept. Swedish philosopher Lennart Nordenfelt points to the fact that most "holistic" theories of health have been concerned about health as a feeling of well-being and a capacity for action (or in the case of ill health, suffering or lack of ability to take action). There is thus a strong conceptual connection between a state of well-being and the ability to act. A person who cannot realize her individual goals may be said to be in an unhealthy state. In this sense, "health" and "disease" may come to belong to different categories. A person may be objectively defined as ill and may even to some extent subjectively know she has some kind of illness, but as long as this suffering does not affect her vital goals in life, Nordenfelt argues, she has a degree of health. "A human being taken as a whole can have a higher or lower degrees of ill health—that is, be more or less able to act relative to his or her goals" (Nordenfelt, 1991a, p. 83 [my translation]).

HEALTH, CULTURE, AND LIFESTYLE

When anthropologists look at how different cultures handle such concepts as health and disease, they focus on how culture informs the interpretation we make of the signals from our body. Drawing on the linguistic repertoire available within a culture, we are socialized into a certain way of categorizing our bodily symptoms. Symptoms that in one culture may be seen as part of normal life circumstances may be classified as symptoms of disease in another culture (Sachs, 1993).

I want to add a few points to this discussion. As I said earlier, one of the problems with a medical concept of illness is its individualistic and biological emphasis, which has led to a division of medical care from other sectors of society. Whenever health, rather than illness, has again become the issue, we have looked at the broader picture of culture and lifestyle to see how they influence our way of taking care of ourselves. As David Aldridge wrote, health has a performative side (Aldridge, 1996). "Health behavior" is something we perform through systematically influencing our life quality. We care not just about our eating habits and the maintenance of our bodies but increasingly also about our cultural behavior: how we spend our time in a broad sense; how we manage our lives; how we attach ourselves to values, other people, and groups; how we seek meaning through, for instance, music. When performing health becomes a lifestyle, people want to signal their identity through the performance values related to health and life quality. Good health becomes a marker of a certain lifestyle, a way of showing others that we care about our bodies and habits of life.

From this perspective, it become important to identify cultural issues when medicine and health performance are discussed. As we know from other fields of study, these somewhat obscure cultural factors play an important role, such as when a company wants to explain why certain strategies work and others do not, or when a certain "culture of learning" affects the ability of students to learn how to learn.

Culture, in other words, is not only a field of society, a certain type of activity (music) in which we engage. The opposite, all-inclusive definition of culture—as a way of living—may also be too broad to really catch the operating factors behind a certain situation. Culture, rather, could be seen as a certain strategy for interpreting symbols or signs, a way to give meaning to the world around us. Culture is not a specific artifact or general way of living informed by a special group. Cultural performance is linked to the individual's situatedness, a way of perceiving and giving meaning to the world informed by a certain perspective. This perspective is rooted in the private life world of the person.

When culture is seen in this way, it may help us overcome the sometimes unhappy divide between "high" and "low" culture, which implies that so-called high culture sometimes has gained priority in the repertoire of those institutions and organizations that want to promote "art and culture" in hospitals. When culture is linked to a certain way of handling or interpreting symbols and situations in a broad sense, we will always have to consider the special context, situatedness, life world, or social position of the person in question. This means that much that is presented in the name of art may have little significance as raw material for building an identity and lifestyle. On the other hand, people may find much meaning in performing cultural activities grounded in their idiosyncratic life situation.

HEALTH RESOURCES, IDENTITY, AND QUALITY OF LIFE

Israeli medical sociologist Aaron Antonovsky (1991) has been working for a long time to clarify the connections between health and how we cope with life. As founder of what he calls "salutogenetic research," his concern is why we maintain health. In contrast to much medical research, the main preoccupation of which is pathogenesis, or why we become sick, Antonovsky seeks to trace our general resources of resistance to disease. The resources are present in all of us, possibly in various degrees. In conceptualizing them, Antonovsky came up with three main components: predictability, conceivability, and meaningfulness. That is, when we feel life to be comprehensible (predictable), manageable (conceivable), and meaningful, we feel coherence and continuity in life. This sense of coherence and continuity seems to favor resistance to disease, according to Antonovsky.

Antonovsky's concept of general resources of resistance is related to the current debate on quality of life, which is spurred by the growing understanding that economic growth and increased material welfare in themselves do not make our experience of life better. Members of different professions, such as psychology and nursing, have suggested, on the basis of their specific knowledge, ways of living that may increase the subjective feeling of a better quality of life. What set of variables might music therapists suggest when *quality of life* is defined?

One of the most influential Scandinavian writers on quality of life has been Norwegian psychologist Siri Næss. According to Næss, quality of life has four main components: (1) activity, which contains the dimensions of engagement, energy, self-realization, and freedom; (2) good interpersonal relations, which are realized through friendship and intimate relations; (3) self-confidence, which has to do with self-esteem and self-acceptance; and (4) a basic sense of happiness, which is maintained through emotional experiences, safety, and joy (see Nordenfelt, 1991a).

Another Norwegian writer, Tone Rustøen, has suggested, from the perspective of nursing science, that such factors as being active, experiencing intersubjectivity, having a feeling of self, and having a basic sense of joy make an important contribution to the quality of life. Rustøen came up with four dimensions that, from her professional background, seemed to be ingredients for a good life: hope, meaning, feelings of communality, and identity (Rustøen, 1991).

Instead of engaging in further debate about various concepts of quality of life, I want to show how this discussion relates to my own findings in my study on music and identity (Ruud, 1997a). What I found when working from the four main categories I used in dealing with material related to musical identity—personal space, social space, the space of time and place, and transpersonal space—was that some of the narratives about musical experiences could not easily be placed into just one category. There were some phenomena that seemed to occur within all four categories. When I looked closer at these categories, I realized that they could be regrouped under another core category: quality of life.

From the current debate about the concept of quality of life, I have become aware that the term refers to a subjective state of meaning, well-being, or happiness, rather than an objective set of criteria that must be fulfilled in order to obtain a certain level of quality of life (see Nordenfelt, 1991a and 1991b). In this sense, it is not sufficient to specify certain necessary material conditions to be met in order to talk about quality of life, although such conditions often strongly influence our life situations. We know that such conditions, as well as many other basic human needs (compare Maslow's hierarchy), are not sufficient to induce a subjective state of "meaning" in life or "happiness." Rather, I would argue that the fact that involvement with music can produce a strong, flexible, and differentiated identity should be regarded as a potential resource in achieving quality of life.

To specify how music may provide such resources, I will explain how I identified a set of four categories. These new categories were *awareness of feelings* (or *vitality*), *agency, belonging,* and *meaning.* As might not surprise us, all significant memories of music seemed to have a certain quality of "affective presence." In other words, the emotional aspects were more or less fore-grounded in the experience. Likewise, I often found that music is linked to a greater awareness of our own possibilities of action, a feeling of mastery, or increased basic social communicative skills. *Belonging* concerned not only aspects of time and place but also our attachment to other people, gender, identity, social positions, ethnicity, or a feeling of belonging within a transcendental real-ity. Significantly, the *meaning* aspects were present in most sto-ries, from the memories of everyday and ordinary experiences to so-called peak experiences. I would say, however, that the experi-ence of having a "strong, flexible, and coherent identity" itself may provide the most basic feeling of meaning in life. By *strong identity,* I mean a concept of self that entails all the above four dimensions of identity. A *flexible identity* implies the ability to compose and adjust a personal narrative in accordance with how life is perceived and lived. A *coherent identity* would imply that I feel continuity and sameness in life. In this sense, I suggest that there are some conceptual relations with what Antonovsky termed "coherence and continuity" and my concept of a "strong, flexible, and coherent identity."

Although my categories have empirical grounding, I do not want to argue for the value of music in a normative sense. As I said earlier, involvement in music is a *potential* resource for obtaining a better quality of life. When we talk about *quality,* we ought to remind ourselves that we are making value judgments along a scale with negative and positive poles (Nordenfelt, 1991a, p. 85). Quality of life can be measured on scales emphasizing, for instance, moral values, intellectual values, or aesthetic values. People place dif-ferent emphasis on different values, and their evaluation of their own goal attainment may vary according to their individual values. This does not mean, however, that music concerns only aesthetic values. We know—especially because of our background in music therapy—that music may be a source of social enrichment and may stimulate communication, intellectual curiosity, and so on.

VITALITY, OR AWARENESS
OF FEELINGS

In my study, I found that from early life on, music contributes greatly to an increased awareness of feelings, an ability to both experience and express feelings. This has to do with the ability to experience emotional nuances, to experience and express various degrees of intensity, and to maintain precise concepts about feelings. This may be considered as having acquired the sense of a basic feeling of vitality—that is, the ability to open oneself to the world, to other people, and to oneself (Monsen, 1991)—an important condition for good personal development. Vitality, then, is a combination of spontaneity and reflexivity. As Norwegian psychologist Jon Monsen writes, vitality has to do with the reciprocity between how we feel and what we do with our feelings in terms of how we experience and express our feelings. Vitality implies our ways of activating a certain range of our feelings, how we integrate our experiences, and how we express them clearly (Monsen, 1991, p. 150).

We could argue that to acquire these emotional resources is an important part of our health, in the sense of having a strong and resistant "self." The opposite case—that is, not having acquired this emotional awareness—is manifested when we can no longer bear our own emotional experiences and try to live in a way that does not activate our feelings. As we know from clinical psychology, we may inhibit and repress our feelings, giving up our self-awareness to protect ourselves against reality. To be more specific, this means that we stop relating to a basic preverbal way of communicating and we cut off the information contained in the feeling. We may lose sight of the nonverbal aspects of our behavior and become estranged from our own self. Other people may find us difficult to perceive and understand. Our energy becomes tied up in our bodies, resulting in a lack of motor flexibility and possibly physiological failure. In some cases, this may even lead to a situation in which we lose the ability to have new personal experiences—we stop interacting with our surroundings (Monsen, 1991, p. 290). In that sense, we may postulate that emotional awareness, or our ability to become aware of ourselves and to reflect on and express emotions, may help us to not to close down.

If we look closer at those situations in which music may engender a greater awareness of feelings, we find narratives in which people reveal several instances of music's being used as a source of activation of feelings, of clarification and expression. An example from work done by Gabrielsson and Lindström (1995) illustrates how music can open us to life:

> About 20 years ago I met with an event that gave me a deep personal shock. This meant that I could not get any contact with people and the life around me. I felt as if I lived in a bell glass with absolute isolation from life. The only thing that reached into myself was music. I was lying in a dark room and listened to music from a gramophone. The music could break through the walls and trickle into me, and I believe that it was the music that meant that I, after a month or two, could begin groping my way into life again (p. 197).

In the same study, Gabrielsson and Lindström (1995) also gave examples of how music could dramatically change one's mood, as in the following:

> I was in a deep depression, but the more I listened to the music, the more my thoughts became lighter. Everything was so sad and the music was so sad to me, but it made me feel more and more that life was coming back (p. 197).

In my own study, I was struck by the awareness of harmony, bodily relaxation, and basic trust that had grown out of the autobiographers' repeated experiences with lullabies, children's tunes, and nursery rhymes throughout childhood. My students easily remembered these melodies and situations and accessed or reproduced the concomitant feelings. I was especially aware of how music had been instrumental in giving children a sense of acceptance, of being met and confirmed in a meaningful situation. Although I read no mentions of musical situations from infancy or the first year of life, I found evidence in the recent literature on interaction theory of how singing or the affective attunement made through tuning in with the child could further the communication of empathy. Knowing that infant interaction can be seen as a series of events based on such musical parameters as time, intensity, and narrative, it seems reasonable to conclude that musical interaction through songs helps to establish a basic sense of intersubjectivity through which a child can, from early on, make an impact on another.

There was also direct emotional awareness in later song situations: the child was able to react to the text of the songs, and there were possibilities for verbal interaction and conceptual clarification by an adult. These situations showed how song texts and larger musical narratives became an arena for training in emotional tolerance and in the ability to contain complex and difficult emotions. There were also examples of songs and singing as a means of emotional and bodily expression.

The narratives showed that later in adolescence, music often became consequential as a source of feeling of authenticity. This feeling may be likened to a sense of having a "real" self, or a self that is felt as natural, "true," or in accordance with how life is experienced in general. In some cases, this also brought a feeling of self-realization, not only in the sense of getting in touch with some inner potential but, as I would rather interpret it, in another sense: through the discovery of a certain music, the individual aligned her identity narrative with a particular belief regarding what life should be like.

It should also be mentioned that strong emotional experiences of music sometimes give us a direct sense of a therapeutic force that stems from the music. As demonstrated in a study by Gabrielsson and Lindström (1995), people sometimes told of the power of music's giving a sense of personal relief and strength that transcended a subjective feeling of being handicapped by physical or mental troubles. The emotional aspect was focused in the moment of a peak experience during listening to music. As was discussed by Gabrielsson and Lindström, these strong experiences were described through such categories of feelings and emotions as "freedom" and "energy." In that study, people often pointed to the therapeutic character of these moments, as in the following: " . . . the tune went straight to my heart, and the hard armor around my feelings opened up and I could both cry and laugh again" (Gabrielsson and Lindström, 1995, p. 199).

If we compare these experiences with the list of "meaningful moments" taken from music therapy situations found in a study by Dorit Amir (1992, pp. 56–58), it seems reasonable to conclude that musical experiences outside the music therapy room are often similar and sometimes have the same effects as those found with the more systematic interventions of the trained music therapist.

This last point leads to a comparison of music therapy and real life experiences. As we know from the theory of music therapy, there is an ongoing discussion about the function of music in therapy—the debate about music *as* therapy versus music *in* therapy. While the former position grants possible therapeutic value to music in and of itself, the latter claims the necessity to ascribe the use of music to some larger psychological or clinical narrative. From the stories I gathered, we might reach either conclusion. Music in itself seems to further a form of emotional cleansing, a way of direct expression of emotion. This way of expressing oneself through music, or living through strong musical experiences, is a way of giving form to emotional expression, although it might be nonverbal. It may hark back to the nonverbal form of expression we used early in life to get in touch with our feelings of vitality (in Daniel Stern's sense). We can also see, however, that narratives about such musical experiences are a sort of personal reflection, discourses on the function of the experience of strong emotions in our own life situations or difficulties.

AGENCY

There is obviously an important aspect of health related to the ability to take responsibility for our own lives and actions, to be able to make choices and follow plans we set. It has been observed that one substantial factor related to our medical culture and our health is a feeling of disempowerment, letting ourselves be managed and treated, often by the extended and sometimes unnecessary use of drugs. An major goal in changing people's lifestyles in favor of self-management of health has to be increasing their sense of agency, of being responsible for their actions.

By the term *agency*, I want to include those aspects of our conduct related to achievement, competency, mastery, and empowerment. The focal concern is how music, or our musical behavior, can influence this aspect of our self-evaluation.

As we know from the performance arena, music can be an important source of the experience of mastery and self-esteem. As I reported in my study, many of the autobiographers had had experiences that made them view themselves as competent people who could enter a social space, take control, and perform. The pleasure of being able to perform on an instrument was prevalent in most autobiographies. Conversely, it was also demonstrated that performance situations, parental pressure, and cultural collision had led to ambivalence, loss of self-confidence, and defeat. I mention this that we may not forget some of the pitfalls of instrumental pedagogy.

As I have argued elsewhere, a preoccupation with music, both listening and performing, may in general contribute to children's development (Ruud, 1975, 1978, 1980a, 1990a; Ruud and Stige, 1994). This concerns all areas of development—emotional, motor, social, cognitive, and ego strength or self-esteem. As part of the basic theory of developmentally oriented music therapy, it is argued that listening to music may help children master the sound environment and achieve new areas of competence. This same may also be true in relation to the sensorimotor skills involved in music-making or some of the basic early social skills involved when people share music. Music-making is not an isolated skill bound to a separate faculty of the mind called "musicality" but a complex behavior involving perception, cognitive skills, motor performance, social communicative skills, and emotional, bodily, and symbolic activity. To be engaged in music means to fully use all these developmental skills. It has been demonstrated by the methodological tools and experiences of the music therapist how development in general can be influenced by music.

In this sense, music can give children an area of competence and prepare them to master and take responsibility for their own conduct. Music empowers us; it gives us a psychological and cultural platform from which to make our own decisions on matters concerning our own lives. When we are engaged in music, we feel we are "somebody"; we gain the right to raise our voices, as my colleague Odd Are Berkaak and I saw in our study of a rock group (see Chapter 6).

One aspect of this empowerment is that music serves as a source of basic social competence. To partake in music through performing, going to concerts, or buying CDs is, in a certain sense, a path to a social life, to paraphrase Ruth Finnegan (1989). As we form our personal music tastes, we enter into dialogues with other people or groups. Through listening to music and engaging in conversation about music with other people, we learn how other people experience music and life in general. Norwegian sociologist Ivar Frønes (1994) termed this aspect of our possibilities of action a "basic social competence." He connects this competence to the ability to decenter oneself—in other words, to take the perspective of others. It is an ability to deconstruct how other people may perceive society, or, regarding music, how certain aesthetics can be evaluated from the context of "the other." This competence is learned simply through identification with artists or through differentiating oneself from others by allying oneself with another broad cultural landscape. We learn to reflect on taste cultures in general as a presupposition for participation in a broader social arena. Through decoding the semiotics of music, we gain social resources and increase our basic social competence.

BELONGING

From a sociological point of view, one of the greatest threats to health and quality of life is the increasing fragmentation of society (Habib, 1994). Modern lifestyles sometimes lead to uprootedness, a breakdown of families, and increased mobility, which in turn lead to a weakening of social networks, individual isolation, and loneliness. When caretaking becomes institutionalized, handicapped people are often marginalized, losing stable relationships and community involvement.

This general sociological picture calls for a massive mobilization of counterforces: we need meeting places where social networks can be established and people can have a sense of belonging. For many, modern organizational life (church groups, volunteer organizations, and leisure activities, such as sports) seems to take care of much of the need to build new relationships and find a place in which to be embedded in a larger cultural setting, but this is not true for everyone.

The public support in Nordic countries for all kinds of grass-roots music activities is an example of how music as a social activity can provide an important conduit for community involvement. Some of the many music venues in which a large percentage of the populations participate are choirs, brass bands, school bands, rock groups, and amateur orchestras.

In interviews I conducted in studying musical autobiographies, it was often the case that music served as an entrée to a social group in which to experience communality and attachments to others. Being with others through music may thus provide intense experiences of involvement, a heightened feeling of being included, a deep relationship with others. Through the intimate frame of musical activity, individuals are bound together through common musical experiences. A choir is a good example: it is a model of the sometimes problematic relationship between the individual and the group.

For people who have been isolated because of their handicap or the "sick role," the music group, or people in the group, may open doors to the larger community. New contacts are established; other people give us access to new values and social experiences. Music becomes a social resource, a way of getting to know groups, communities, and cultures. (See Stige, 1996, for a discussion of a music therapy project in a community specifically aimed at integration.) In this setting, people can come to feel part of a tradition and can form long-term attachments.

Belongingness concerns not only our relationships to other people or larger groups or communities but also our feeling of being at home in the larger world, in history and geography. Our sense of historical identity encompasses our rootedness in history as well as in contemporaneity. Identification with historical music gives us a sense of belonging to a larger historical narrative. Going to concerts or listening to contemporary music gives us a sense of identification with the part of history in which we are personally taking part. This sense of embeddedness in groups, subcultures, and histories could, of course, be extended to ethnicity and nationality (Ruud, 1997a).

MEANING AND COHERENCE

Much of Antonovsky's argument was built around how our sense of coherence and meaning in life can contribute to our general resources for resistance to illness. Of course, our conception of such broad, complex terms as *meaning* and *coherence* will determine what to include in a discussion of this issue. In a broad sense, I find it meaningful to say that a "strong, flexible, and differentiated identity," which encompasses my four dimensions of the personal, social, time/place, and transpersonal, adds content to the categories of meaning and coherence. Here, however, I will discuss only those aspects of involvement in music that seem more directly related to the aspect of meaning, although *meaning*, in the sense that our musical experiences are remembered or felt as being significant, always involves such aspects. This most obviously relates to all discussions concerning emotional and bodily involvement in music. Because our bodies and emotions are involved in most situations in which music creates an "affective presence," this has to be included as a backdrop for this discussion.

After I studied the verbal reports, I later added the category of *transpersonal space*. I got a strong sense of the necessity many individuals feel to experience their lives and existence as part of a larger context. To many people, this sense of meaningful existence was anchored to some larger principles inscribed in religious values or the more humanistic concepts of *humankind, nature,* or *cosmos*.

Meaning was also produced in a sense of well-being obtained through the pleasure of the musical experience. This sense of well-being may very well contribute to the subjective feeling of quality of life as defined by individuals themselves. As we saw in the earlier discussion of quality of life, such a feeling of well-being is not equivalent to a sense of "meaning," which may often include a broader perspective of life: finding that our lives have value (in retrospect) in spite of our present condition. "Meaning" thus includes a sense of wholeness and purpose in life despite physical condition and despite a subjective state of feeling or suffering. It seems to me that music sometimes becomes a reminder of this sense of coherence and purpose; music provides the link to a sense of being included in a context that is "larger than life."

In general, the emotional experience of music seems to help people establish memories and integrate and formulate them in a metaphoric form that gives direction to their personal narratives. Contained within the musical emotional memory is a sense of continuity and sameness in life: sometimes a remembered piece of music functions as a memory bank, as a deposit box for a basic sense of self, an identity feeling, or a strong positive feeling of life. Of course, this is easily linked to a general feeling of meaning in life, but it can also be seen how music could become part of the resources that help us resist illness—in other words, how music can be a means of promoting health.

HEALTH, MUSIC, AND IDENTITY

As I remarked earlier, the categories of *vitality, agency, belonging,* and *meaning* were drawn from my studies on music and identity. In the context of my four parameters of identity (personal space, social space, the space of time and place, and transpersonal space), these categories form the basis of a strong argument for the connection of music to identity and health. If being involved in music generally strengthens our sense of identity and if having a strong and differentiated sense of identity is connected to an higher quality of life, then it follows that music contributes to health in general.

In my theory of musical identity, I emphasized the point that the formation of an identity results from the way people narrate the story of their lives. Drawing on memories of significant life events as they are experienced through music, people plot scripts that organize the events of their lives into coherent narratives. In a certain sense, these scripts are based on certain value scales or world views, as illustrated by the particular metaphors used to create coherence in these stories.

Summing up our lives at a certain point may reveal greater or lesser satisfaction. We may feel that we have realized some of our basic values or vital goals. This view of life can be described as a sense of equilibrium between life as a whole and present conditions

(Nordenfelt, 1991a, p. 44). This is how Nordenfelt defines *happiness,* which he places at the core of his concept of quality of life.

I am well aware that the sometimes generality of my argument may be considered a weakness. On the other hand, I have tried to synthesize some of the experiences of others in the field of music therapy and my own research on music and identity within the frame of a broader cultural outlook on the role of music in society. Within the context of today's emphasis on health and culture, the lessons of music therapy may be a good starting point for understanding how cultural activities can contribute to the quality of life and a subjective sense of health.

Chapter 5

THE CONCEPT OF *MUSIC*
IN IMPROVISATIONAL
MUSIC THERAPY

A central issue in the theory of music therapy is whether we can talk about the therapeutic qualities of music itself or must merely use music as a means to obtain goals specified by various developmental or psychotherapeutic theories. This conflict is rooted in the history of music therapy itself, or more specifically, in the conflict raised by modern music therapy's facing its historical roots. As I have written elsewhere, music therapy may take its methods and goals from the theoretical models of other treatment modalities, or it may be necessary to view our field in a larger cultural, societal, or philosophical context (Ruud, 1980b, 1990b, 1990c). In itself, the fact that my book *Music Therapy and Its Relationship to Treatment Theories* has been translated into several languages proves that music therapists recognize this conflict.

The alliance between music therapy and other therapeutic systems may seem rather obvious to most contemporary music therapists, especially those concerned with its measurable aspects or those heavily into psychodynamic theory. There are still many, however, who insist on emphasizing the therapeutic qualities inherent in music. These are the clinicians who say that it is the mere experience of music that leads to results.

Kenneth Bruscia (1987) explicitly formulated the issue of therapy versus music as "music *in* therapy" versus "music *as* therapy." Although he does not want to disclaim the former position, especially because he broadly outlined improvisational models himself, he views the essence of music therapy as the use of music *as* therapy. Gary Ansdell (1995), writing from the vantage point of Creative Music Therapy, also makes this distinction, using additional theoretical arguments and clinical evidence of the power of music in itself. Of course, there are many more who could be added to this list. I remember that one day in Phoenicia, New York, Helen Bonny remarked, after having read my book *Music Therapy and Its Relationship to Current Treatment Theories* (Ruud, 1980b), that she disagreed with its basic intent. She held that music could stand on its own feet. Having participated in a Guided Imagery and Music (GIM) session with one of her colleagues, Sara Jane Stokes, the following day, I can see her point. My first GIM experience was quite powerful to me. The music took me right to some sensitive areas of my life history. I was impressed by the musical journey. Of course, this one trip did not make any psychological or "therapeutic" changes, although my views about the power of transcendental experiences were changed forever.

THE MEANING OF MUSIC
IN MUSIC THERAPY

There is no agreement about the nature of music in music therapy. Adherents of various schools of music therapy understand music differently, more or less consistent with the underlying values of their particular theoretical tradition. For example, in behavioral or learning theories, music in therapy is handled as a reinforcement tool, and music is sometimes deconstructed in acoustics laboratories to reveal its physical nature. There are also other more functional views of the role of music in therapy: as a discriminatory stimulus, as a medium for conveying a message, as a frame for a learning situation, and so forth. It seems inconsistent with the behavioral tradition, though, to engage too deeply in speculation about what music should mean, signify, or communicate.

Such aspects of music in therapy are grounded more in its humanistic and analytical traditions. Here, we often find descriptions of music as a language, as a means of emotional expression, as a way of communicating a nonverbal message. Because of philosophical and methodological considerations, the nature of music is verbally reconstructed through phenomenological descriptions, subjective statements, or more speculative (in the positive sense) aesthetic considerations.

Other traditions in our field may base their philosophy on the assumption that music is, in the end, a vehicle for expressing something "absolute," something basic to our concept of life or our cosmic reality. A look at history will tell us that this representation is rooted in the romantic philosophy of art. Throughout the nineteenth century, the aesthetics of music became part of the ideology that would form a strong defense against the emerging natural-science understanding of reality (Østerberg, 1995). Recent research into the philosophy of music has reconstructed or deconstructed the grand narrative about musical representation that started with Rousseau. The point of departure seems to have been the belief in music's ability to make reality "more real" than could be sensed directly (Wikshåland, 1995): today, this belief seems to have dissolved in the face of the modern stance that it is impossible to express oneself outside of cultural and linguistic forms.

We have lately seen how a romantic image of music as a universal kind of therapy or peacemaker has won popularity, because of such factors as changing concepts of science, a more holistic approach to life, influences from other music cultures, and increased understanding of the breakdown of linear logic or instrumental reasoning. A recent change in the scientific climate appears to favor a paradigmatic change in the field of music therapy in which emphasis is once on the metaphysical powers of music to effect change regardless of the therapeutic interventions made by the therapist. A characteristic feature of this view seems to be a belief that music can illustrate some of the basic characteristics of "the universe," "reality," or whatever we name the world "out there."

Two rather opposite world views might be reached as a consequence of this holistic approach. In response to the weakness of rational thought, some theorists have adopted a religious attitude beyond art and science in order to seek a new understanding of reality. Such an attitude implies an understanding of or a search for another reality behind what is commonly known. One corollary of this view, which stems from the late eighteenth century, is a belief that this "more real" reality, of which we all are a common part, can be shared through music, for instance. Such statements as "Music is the ultimate leap" or "We all are part of a universal vibration" may derive from this interpretation. It is hard to see, however, how this universal partaking—through music—in this other reality could guarantee peace, health, and harmony unless there are some outer forces that intervene in the more trivial affairs that disrupt our life. If there are such directive forces, this view is more mechanistic (rather than holistic) than the most hard-core natural-science music therapy.

Instead of asking if music represents another kind of reality, a reality that is "more real" and more conducive to producing health, we ought to ask what kind of mythology is producing this kind of ideology. Furthermore, we should ask if this mythology is useful in promoting health. Perhaps it is. If the mentality of the question implies a more holistic outlook toward health, then we might be able to use music in a more prophylactic, preventive way. That is, if it views health not only as a biological question but also as one concerning the personal, social, and economic aspects of humankind, and if it means sticking to an antireductionist attitude, a way of maintaining the complexity of the question of music's influence on humankind and the use of this influence in a therapeutic discourse, then perhaps it is useful.

Among current concepts of music we will also find some that point to the mere texture of music and how music itself makes possible a form of perception, a certain poetics, that extends and clarifies the borders between fantasy and reality. From such a phenomenological view, music's temporal quality makes possible its therapeutic use.

I do not think it is possible to reach a consensus about the nature of music in music therapy. My aim of this essay is rather to discuss some of the many concepts of music. Some years ago, I was struck by the deceptively simple question asked by my colleague Odd Are Berkaak, a Norwegian anthropologist: "Why does music mean what it means?" Coming from a department of musicology, I was used to taking for granted that this question should be answered by looking at music—at musical details in a musical context—or by studying music and perception together, as advocated by, for instance, Leonard B. Meyer in *Emotion and Meaning in Music.* My anthropologist friend, however, took another stand: music means different things to different people because of their specific cultural and biographical backgrounds. He meant that in order to grasp how we define and understand the nature of music, we have to look at the broader nonmusical context of people making judgments about music. Bringing an anthropologist into the field of music therapy would mean, then, to study how cultural factors—how ideologies and practices within a particular context come to influence a culture's view or construction of music.

This idea is easy to accept when we read anthropological reports about music in foreign cultures, cultures of "the others." It is my impression, however, that this idea is met with some reluctance when applied to the field of music therapy. Music therapists—particularly those concerned with music as a communication tool—have a hard time giving up the idea that music in some way mirrors or expresses people's inner nature in an immediate, transparent way. Music, emotion, and body form a strong defense against intruding deconstructive ideas.

AGAINST ESSENTIALISM?

There are two interconnected forms of essentialism that keep popping up in the field of music therapy. First, we find the idea that there is some meaning inherent in music itself that we can grasp by listening thoroughly to it or analyzing its transcription. It is important, however, to differentiate between what we term the "poetic" or aesthetic quality of music and what has been called "the absolute." This distinction is significant because the idea of "the absolute" in music, according to German musicologist Carl Dahlhaus's historical interpretation, would imply a strong metaphysical bent, where the "absolute" often has been seen as the "eternal," "infinite," or "all-encompassing" (Dahlhaus, 1978). Although we may say that music expresses "something," music is not a language in the same sense that a verbal language is. From the perspective of information theory, we may say that music, understood as a particular organization or categorization of sounds, displays "differences" that in turn give rise to "information." Information regarded as a difference does not imply, however, that these sounds are given a fixed meaning. The kind of meaning we read into the differences varies, not only on the basis of structural aspects of the music but also on the basis of the biographical-cultural context of the musical reception. Before these "differences" are rewritten and represented in some system of meaning and before the aesthetic experience is represented in language, however, it should be possible to talk about music as something "absolute" in a musical sense.

The question is, however, whether such a view is only theoretical, because it seems impossible to communicate without using language. In trying to state something about "the absolute," we often run into the paradox about which Adorno (1978) reminded us in his discussion of the linguistic character of music: music is similar to language, he wrote, in that its figures may become signlike through a process in which music absorbs certain characteristics of signals. This "second nature" of music is what Adorno confronts with "the absolute" in music, the level at which we play with significations.

It is still possible, then, to hold a perspective on music that allows for all kinds of projections. As long as this perspective is at a level of the absolute, a level not reached by words, we can postulate that music is a language of the body, through gestures and so on. We could say that there is a major difference between a dogmatic discourse that states, for instance, that music is an expression of "the infinite" and a discourse that attempts to argue for the possibility that music can carry multiple meanings.

The second form of essentialism we may find in the idea that music is an expression of some "deep inner" state of the client/therapist-composer when it is improvised or an expression of the genius of the composer when we listen to precomposed music. This stance is somewhat modified by the following argument: because it is obvious that musical expression sounds different from the verbal or emotional expression through which we usually communicate, it is said that music may more be an expression of the logical form (Langer, 1953) of the emotion than of the emotion itself. In other words, we could say that music is the symbolic form and the content is emotion.

Let us consider the view of music as some kind of mirror of inner states, as a way of expressing these states. For music therapy, such a view would be of much help in explaining how music helps the "unspeakable inner" come out and would make a good rationale for the use of music in therapy.

In the language of semiotics, music is a kind of sign. For the music therapist, music could even be regarded as a "motivated" sign—that is, a sign in which the role of cultural convention is minor. If music is a motivated sign, it may be something we all can "read" without knowledge of the conventions or rules that connect the sign's form and content. In semiotics, a sign has two sides: both a content (signifié) and an expression (signifiant). Within such a theoretical frame, it could be advocated that music therapists read the content of the sign—that is, the emotional message from the client. If we believe that emotions are biological states with more or less universal features, music therapists "read" rather than "interpret" what clients try to express in therapy.

In the semiotics of music, there are two types of signs relevant to this discussion: index and icon. In the index form, the sign's content is linked to the way it is expressed in a causal manner; for example, the sound of a running horse is an index that informs us both about the horse and the type of ground it is running on. We may similarly think about types of musical indexes, such as so-called indexes of states. These may be seen as symptoms that suggest something about a mental or physical state, such as screaming, sobbing, or crying. We sometimes observe clinical situations in which clients sing about their emotional pain, and musical expression from time to time takes the form of "sobbing." This may be the closest we come to considering a musical expression as an "index of state." Are these situations only exceptions, however?

More often, music therapists encounter a form of musical sign called an "icon." An icon differs from the index in the sense that it has no causal connection to the first incident the way smoke has to fire or a footprint, to a foot. One example would be when music is perceived as expressing an emotion but we do not have the necessary information to interpret what it is the client is trying to express. Content and expression are tied together through similarity. Because there is no causal relation, music semioticians may say that the relation between the expression and the content to some extent is arbitrary. Theorists may disagree, however, to the extent that culture and conventions influence the way the emotion is expressed or how we interpret the icon. If we say that "icons of states" are icons of "indexes of states," we could say that the "index of states" supplies a raw material of emotionally motivated gestures that are represented in stylized form within an "icon of state." In other words, our body and feelings may be imprinted on the gestural form of the musical expression. This means, furthermore, that although clients' musical styles are highly idiosyncratic, we, as music therapists, should be able to trace the underlying "state of feeling."

This argument, which to some extent strongly supports an expressionist assumption in music aesthetics—that is, that music is seen as an expression of human feelings—is somewhat controversial in music aesthetics. This view has led some theorists to regard music as some kind of emotional alphabet and to try to reconstruct the hermeneutic rules as a kind of instruction manual to be used by the listener or interpreter. I am not sure if this debate is relevant to our discussion. When music therapists work with improvisation, there is some likelihood that the musical "language" more directly reflects the emotional state of the people involved. When they work with recorded music, and when the "chain of communication" is distorted by history, technology, and the context of reception, the discussion is a different one.

Is there further evidence to support our argument that an improvised musical statement made in therapy can be heard and correctly interpreted as an "icon of state" of the client's inner life? Some years ago, Australian researcher Manfred Clynes (1977) proposed that music is a kind of "sentic mirror" of genetically preprogrammed emotional states. He supported his theory with cross-cultural experiments showing that so-called sentic states are universal and are reflected in musical expression (signifiant). I felt uneasy about this theory because of following reasons. Emotional categories would have to be differently coded or represented in different cultures. Although sadness, for instance, may be universally felt, the way it is expressed would have to differ from culture to culture. Clynes's study challenged this view. Furthermore, although these emotions are represented in various cultures, their cultural meaning would differ. This last view is supported by studies of the anthropology of emotions.

Clynes tried to show how emotions, or sentic states, could be expressed through a "sounding contour," a tonal and temporal dynamic, rather than through a concrete melodic-rhythmic formula. In other words, a slowly downward-moving chromatic melodic line represents sadness (or melancholy in Purcell and Dowland's cultural landscape). When Clynes demonstrated how this "sounding contour" actually sounds, however, he came close to the melodic formula of the baroque formula for sadness. A good example he gives is the lament from Purcell's *Dido and Aeneas*. A more puzzling example, I would add, is the Beatles' "My Guitar Gently Weeps."

Perhaps this is a crucial point. The contour of the melodic line, along with the tempo, points not to a categorical feeling, such as sadness, but to a "vitality affect" in Daniel Stern's sense. Through the processes of amodal perception, we can infer an emotional state from a sound contour. Put otherwise, because of the perceived similarity of the two domains, we can let one function as a metaphor for the other. The musical sounds may become metaphors for the affects felt, or the affects may come to represent the movement-shapes of the sounds.

CODE COMPETENCY
AND THE DISCOURSE ON MUSIC

As I argued earlier, the question "What is music?" cannot be answered independent of any theoretical tradition. When music psychologists and acousticians answer this question, they often focus on how music is made up of single tones that can be studied for their frequency, amplitude, and pitch. Philosophers and aestheticians point to music's more phenomenological characteristics, whereas sociologists try to solve the problem by defining music the way people in general do.

If we accept the postmodern position that there is no "true" way to answer our question, that no one theoretical tradition is more basic than any other, we must choose more pragmatic arguments to defend any particular definition of music. I argue that music consists of sounds primarily characterized through being perceived as signs with meaning. One reason for choosing this definition is because it allows us to study the interaction between how signs or sounds are organized and the social, cultural, or biographical processes that give these signs meaning. This means that I understand the question of meaning and signification in music as a relational phenomenon, something that cannot be explained by looking only at music itself or by studying music only from the perspective of the listener.

Instead of reducing sounds to regular vibrations, I choose to view them as the smallest unreducible entities. We can perceive innumerable sounds, detect differences in sounds, and organize sounds into shorter or longer sequences. Because we select some sounds as more important than others and, as a presupposition, perceive that some of these sounds can be meaningfully combined in certain ways, I suppose they are perceived as cultural entities—that is, as signs. Such signs are organized into larger entities: tunes, works, or improvisations.

Even if sounds, in becoming cultural entities, can never be perceived as "empty" signs, we react to these signs with varying degrees of competence. We read them differently, regarding both meaning and our expectations about internal connections between them. In addition, we have acquired varying degrees of competence in decoding sundry extramusical meanings. The intra- and extramusical meanings of signs follow the rules of a particular code. The first code we probably learn in life is the rule that tells us how musical sounds are truly different from other sounds. Research also indicates that infants are born with the ability to perceive the difference between sounds organized as music and those organized into words (Fiske, 1993). Soon after learning that rule, we learn codes that inform us which and how sounds can be linked to carry specific expectations. Because this learning always happens within a specific social or cultural context, codes also inform us about what these signs mean, or rather what kind of sociocultural reality they refer to. In other words, we learn conventions that inform us about the connection between a musical style and extramusical symbolism.

So far, I have emphasized the languagelike character of music—our tendency to perceive music as some message being transmitted between participants in a musical transaction. Something happens to the message, however, when I describe it in words. What has been wordless and polysemous is now bound to language in an attempt to conceptualize and verbally clarify it. As I said earlier, though, before music has been written into our conceptual world, we can speak about the aesthetic quality of music.

This aesthetic or poetic quality belongs to a level of meaning that can be regarded as a perceptual field, as sounding patterns that capture our attention when unfolding in time and space. This is music in the present tense before the experience is represented by linguistic categories. Such music cannot be described, except in musical sound terms, without losing its sense of the present. Verbal transcriptions place it in the past. All such linguistic representations have a relative value in relation to the actual sounds of music. No such description or representations can claim absolute validity; that is, no one can say "music is really" so and so.

Our encounters with music may result in aesthetic experiences. It is such experiences that we try to formulate in words, to give a name. This categorization sometimes results in a coherent theory, an aesthetic theory—or for music therapists, in a rationale for the value or role of music in therapy. This process of categorization does not follow, of course, as a reflex of musical structure, but is driven by certain ideas about music. In this sense, we can say that our manner of talking about music makes visible how our discourse on music is embedded in a larger theoretical or ideological field.

The fact that music can produce experiences we find difficult to put into words is an important characteristic of music or aesthetic messages in general. An aesthetic experience produced by music implies the possibility of creating a new category of experience, of experiencing the world in a new way. For music therapy, this seems one of the most basic rationales for the use of music.

When we give a name to an aesthetic experience, we also make an explicit value judgment. At the same moment we represent our experience by naming it, we make concrete and tangible something that had been hidden to others, something incommunicable. Music becomes a structure that carries into the world this something, to which we can point and give a name. The unsaid is put into words. At that same moment, however, music is conventionalized and given the character of verbal language.

In the process of making this "unspeakable space" by carrying the unspeakable into verbal discourse, we write the aesthetic experience into a cultural context. The aesthetic experience becomes part of a social interaction and a cultural theme. The very naming of the experience becomes an utterance about a value, an attempt to situate the unspeakable within a larger cultural community. The naming of the experience is no longer an explication of an experience; it is now given place in social space, within a larger cultural context. This "placing" becomes a marker of position in social space. The conceptualization becomes a cultural theme. Thus, we can read aesthetics as both an explication of and materialization of cultural themes.

One explanation sometimes given for why we never can describe the "true" nature of music and musical experiences is our situatedness within a language, a linguistic code, that always mediates the world for us. This stance is in line with that of the recent philosophical bent of hermeneutics, which has been described as a continuation of and reaction against the traditional hermeneutics of Schleiermacher and Dilthey. This philosophical or ontological orientation, first proposed by Heidegger and Gadamer, generally holds that all knowledge or perception is modulated by language and is marked by time and history. This thesis has radical consequences for the way philosophical hermeneutics regards understanding. We can never see something in a historical vacuum; we always view things from a perspective that is formed by the past and carries an implicit interest about the future. We always perceive something as "something" (Gilje, 1987, p. 22).

This is why, as I claimed earlier, our linguistic representation of music not only refers to music itself but also has been chosen with regard to where we place ourselves in relation to values, norms, and myths. In other words, a study of the ways we talk about music could reveal that the words and categories we choose when we rewrite or represent music serve to delimit ourselves. We can regard all discussions about music as a way to make explicit value-laden negotiations between us and "them."

If we accept such a radical hermeneutic standpoint, we must discern context and intention to be able to understand the concept of music that is advocated. By context, I mean that it is the very situation in which our concept of music is being used that makes the actual use of the concept understandable. This implies that the convention we use when we speak about aesthetic experiences is a kind of aesthetic practice. Norwegian philosopher Kjell Johannessen described this practice, as did Ludwig Wittgenstein, as a rule-following practice (Ruud, 1992b). This implies that we should pay more attention to the ways people *use* aesthetic terms than to the linguistic terms themselves. To understand what is implied in an aesthetic statement, we have to grasp the situation in which language is used, its complicated character, and implicit tacit knowledge. An aesthetic practice implies mastering a certain repertoire of situations in which aesthetic terms are used. To master a language, according to Wittgenstein, means to master a reality. To master the use of language in aesthetic contexts implies mastering manifold attitudes, skills, and presuppositions that together create an aesthetic reality. It is also important to grasp that the very formation of the concepts that constitute this aesthetic reality constitutes the aesthetic experience. In other words, there is a relationship between the use of language and the aesthetic experience.

This again must be understood in the same sense in which Wittgenstein proposed how words gain meaning through the context in which they are used. How words are used in practice gives them meaning. Wittgenstein's description of "something that we know when no one asks us but no longer know when we are supposed to give an account of it" (Wittgenstein, 1967, p. 42; see also Ruud, 1992b, p. 228) is as well suited to music as it is to linguistic expressions. This implies that our knowledge of music is a kind of proficiency or skill.

When I said earlier that intention is also important to understanding a certain concept of music, I meant that we choose a particular concept of music to give music a certain function or to justify a certain practice. Music is communication and interaction, music therapists claim. In so doing, they provide a concept of music that argues in favor of a certain therapeutic use of music.

MUSIC THERAPY
AS A SOCIAL FIELD

To understand why our private translations of music are part of the culture and society we live in, we must consider how different genres of music relate to one other. Sociologist Howard Becker described how we move through different art worlds when we visit art exhibitions, go to the theater, or attend concerts. Each of these arenas demands a different skill or convention from us: how to look, interpret, appreciate, or behave in general is learned through participation.

If we transpose this view to the arena of music, we can see how society's experience of music is itself governed by different conventions. We know there are different ways to learn and practice music. Concerts may be held in various settings, each of which has its own dress code, rituals for preparation and closure, and rules for behavior during performances and intermissions. We may find divergent opinions about what is an ugly sound versus a beautiful sound, about how music should be composed and performed, and so on (see Becker, 1982). I am sure that if we look at the field of music therapy, we will find a similar variety of conventions among music therapists about what to play, how to approach the client with music, which genres are appropriate, which aesthetic is valid and true, and so forth.

Seeing music as a set of conventions may help us view the various genres with the distance necessary to detect significant similarities and differences. A theory of conventions does not, however, capture the dynamics in or between diverse art worlds. French cultural sociologist Pierre Bourdieu suggested considering separate areas of society as social fields; art, for example, is the field of symbolic production. A field is an area in which a group of people and/or institutions struggle with something they have in common. We struggle with values, about the right to participate in the field, about the right to partake and to have influence, and to obtain dominant positions. A field is recognizable by its dynamics, by its steady movement. Within a field, we find both orthodox and heterodox followers, the latter of whom challenge the dominant theory.

The concept of *field* must be understood within Bourdieu's theory of "habitus" and "cultural capital" (Bourdieu, 1984, 1990). The expression *symbolic capital,* which can be understood when contrasted with the more widely used term *economic capital,* concerns the appropriation of cultural goods, or the ability to make ourselves at home in the dominating culture—among those who rule classical music, literature, and art; those who have acquired the ability to express themselves in a "cultivated" manner; or those who graduated from certain universities. This is not the case only in French culture. In most Western societies and educational systems, cultural capital is transferred from one generation to the next—while the system tries to hide the significance of the transfer. Another term used lately is *information capital*. Whatever term we use, however, the consequences for our society of the actuality behind the concept are the same. Information capital and economic capital are connected: we often find those who have much of one or the other in positions of power.

If we take the perspective that participation in music is participation in a social field, we see the struggle between genres: classical music versus popular music, folk music versus commercial music, and so on. We may also find that the symbolic capital tied to classical music has greater prestige, garnering it more money from private sponsors and governments. At the same time, those engaged in such power struggles may be mystified by the elevation of classical music to the position of an "absolute music," one that is, so to speak, exempt from the everyday.

Bourdieu meant his concept of *habitus* to connote a "system of more or less endurable dispositions," a kind of social competence founded in the body that we acquire throughout childhood in relation to a certain class, gender, and so forth. By appropriation a certain musical culture, we appropriate a bodily disposition, a way of being that seems natural. This knowledge is of consequence to music therapists in the sense that through our music choices and our ways of being in our bodies, we communicate values that are not always are in accordance with the life views of our clients.

Chapter 6

POPULAR MUSIC
AND THE AESTHETICS
OF EVERYDAY LIFE

Music therapists often work within a musical idiom that sets them apart from the general music of their society. Some of them live in their own musical culture with specially composed music and selected "therapeutic" instruments or idiosyncratic improvisational methods, creating a context in which there is meaning only in the boundaries of the therapeutic setting. Other therapists draw heavily from the traditional classical music tradition or work with popular and folk-music idioms relevant to their client population.

Because music therapists are not obsessed with the same missionary zeal we sometimes find in music educators, this situation is similar to the prevalent postmodern music scene in contemporary society. In this chapter, however, I want to focus on the use of popular music in music therapy. A better understanding of how a particular genre is situated in a larger music cultural field can help us improve communication with our clients, especially adolescents. As many music therapists have found, there are also resources in popular music that can help bring out a feeling of mastery and empowerment in the young, furthering the process of social integration and enhancing a feeling of community—of being part of a social network, as I argued in previous chapters.

The study I will present later in this chapter came out of a 3-year research project conducted in a suburb of Oslo, Norway, with social anthropologist Odd Are Berkaak of the University of Oslo. Between 1988 and 1991, we followed a rock group to rehearsals, parties, concerts, tours, and the recording studio. The research process was similar that used by anthropologists studying foreign music cultures. One important difference, however, is that we conducted our project in our contemporary culture, studying a musical form familiar to most people. The method of research was participant observation, together with extensive interviews with band members and the larger music network. We did historical research, listening to old tapes produced by the band and trying to read everything written about the band. We interviewed parents, teachers, youth workers, and record companies (as far away as Los Angeles). We also made a 45-minute video (with professional help) and wrote a book (Berkaak and Ruud, 1992).

Although the study was not a music therapy project, I have included it in this book, hoping to show how rock and roll can be a social resource for integrating its participants into the local community, establishing a network of musicians that extends to the national level. We found that the mastering of popular music codes became a symbolic resource that helped participants to maintain meaning and control in daily life and furthered the development of a strong identity anchored in a local musical aesthetics rooted in the hard-rock groove. We undertook the project to study how musical and cultural processes interact in a modern urban environment and how a specific musical or symbolic (meaning-based) community actually perceived the world—that is, how their basic values and ideologies informed their music aesthetics, experience, and expression. Before I present our findings, however, let us discuss the role of music and aesthetics as they are understood from the perspective of youth studies, ethnography of popular music, and cultural studies.

THE HEADPHONE GENERATION

Modern electronic media have made music a part of everyday life. In concerts and listening activities, through films, through videos, through advertisements, in performing, through headphones that let us carry our music with us as our private portable soundtrack, music contextualizes our lives and is itself contextualized. The music industry distributes sounds and music as raw materials for the production of symbols. As symbols, music is locally and privately received and reworked, remixed, or recombined. It could be generally stated that the result is that music is constructed as a means of mapping a complex contemporaneity. Music integrates our lives vertically, as a significant part of life history. Performing and listening to music necessarily involve a symbolic work (Willis, 1990) related to remembering significant events, the formation of collective and local history, and the founding of space and place (Berkaak and Ruud, 1994). Music is used as a social resource for everything from a conversational base, to network-building, to a means for negotiating values (for instance, authenticity and ideologies of aesthetics, technology, ethnicity, and gender). It could be said that music generally has become an important part of the "resources people have for identifying selves and persons in a specific culture" (Harré and Gillett, 1994).

It could be said that the generation that grew up between the 1970s and 1990s heard more music before they went to school than their grandparents heard during their whole lives. We might call this generation the "headphone generation," socialized in a soundscape in which popular music, as both foreground and background, colored everyday life. For this generation, music has always been present, in everyday rituals, as a cassette player baby-sitting them while their parents did housework, and during hours of listening to CDs and film music and watching music videos.

One of the most significant changes in recent history has been our relationship with music, or our music habits, a change recorded in most quantitative music sociology studies. Young people commonly spend several hours a day listening to music. The Walkman phenomenon is fairly recent; the device that lets us carry our music with us was conceived by Sony president Akio Morita during a walk in New York in 1980. The Walkman and its clones have made possible what British cultural sociologist Ian Chambers described as the nomadism of modernity "in which music on the move is continually being decontextualized and recontextualized in the inclusive acoustic and symbolic life of everyday life" (Chambers, 1990, p. 2).

The question is, what does this change mean? What does it mean to be able to move around in a changing soundscape embedded in our private soundtracks—or musical autobiographies—that colors our horizons of expectations? What is the function of music when it is drawn into our everyday life, as a soundtrack for activities of everyday life?

MUSIC AS A MAP
OF REALITY

From the point of view of new so-called critical musicology, it could be said that traditional musicology has not contributed much to the formulation of a concept of music that would clarify the meaning of music in our media-saturated society. Musicologists often take an analytical stance in which detailed probing into the parameters of music often makes music uninteresting to other researchers. The extreme technicality of much musicological research has even led other researchers to approach music with embarrassment because they lack formal knowledge of music theory. Music plays a central part, however, in many media and youth studies, and the study of popular music is an institutionalized international discipline. In fact, some of the most enlightening treatments of music come from this new interdisciplinary approach to the study of music (see Middleton, 1990).

An effect of a strong musicological paradigm has been that music often is treated as an autonomous object, essentialized in the sense that its meaning and significance is seen as residing in its structure. Musicologists try to read music's meaning by closely describing its structure, a practice that ethnomusicologist Christopher Waterman named "learned animism" (Waterman, 1990). They further try to capture the nature of music in categories and concepts derived from the study of classical music. In this sense, they try to colonize all forms of music into their own theoretical frameworks, models, or canonic categories. Recently, this tendency has met with strong criticism, especially from feminist musicology, which has made problematic the very metaphysical or epistemological background of such research. The statement made by leading feminist musicologist Susan McClary—"I am no long sure what *music* is"—thus created the moral panic among music researchers necessary to initiate a search for other ways of conceptualizing music (McClary, 1991, p. 19). Symptomatic of this new turn is the recent statement made by John Shepherd (1993), one of the leading researchers in popular music:

> Music's materiality functions as a medium of placement and as an instrument of power at the same time as it encapsulates and articulates established patterns of social relations. The

materiality of music positions and structures, but not in a determining fashion. People position and structure sounds as much as they are positioned and structured by them (p. 173).

This statement is very far removed from Shepherd's earlier position, so typical of a lot of work in the sociology of music in the 1970s and 1980s, when the structure of music was seen as mirroring the structure of society (the so called homology model). At the same time, Shepherd's statement admits the difficulty of making general statements about the role and meaning of music by letting the theoretical concept of "position" act on the object of study. It is exactly this discursively inscribed *indeterminacy* of music, or what I earlier called the transitional nature of music, that methodologically creates difficulties when we study its effects. Concurrently, this indeterminate nature—this polysemous quality—may account for the important role music plays in today's media society.

An alternative concept of music could portray music as something into which histories and traditions are inscribed or encoded, something into which we write our life experiences, an object we act toward to articulate values and ideas. Maybe the best way to understand the role of music in the media or for the young consumer is to state that music is a map of life forms and realities. In developing this metaphor of music as a map, I will postulate that music

- Has a sign structure and a sign history, a certain materiality (which may be sometimes most adequately described by traditional musicology)
- Consists of signs always decoded from a specific context— a personal autobiography, historical situation, cultural position, or interpretative community
- Creates a space for presence, a space into which we can project and articulate values

If we start with this discursive concept of music, we may be able to probe some relationships between music and everyday life, to dismantle the role of music as an overall system of symbols in society. Taking this idea further, we can state, as I have said, that there is a connection between music and identity, that music has become one of the resources people have for identifying and construing identities. We can begin our study of this process of identity construction with how these resources are put to work in the coordinated actions of the episodes of everyday life. We can look at how people produce the psychological phenomena of those agreed-on versions of the past called "memories," which they describe using the appropriate resources (see Harré and Gillett, 1994, p. 98).

EVERYDAY AESTHETICS
AS NECESSARY SYMBOLIC WORK

It has been argued that in today's industrialized, commercialized society, people do not find meaning and personal fulfillment in their real jobs. Instead, leisure time is transformed into a kind of necessary symbolic work through which people transform and appropriate situations, norms, and values to serve their own cultural interests (Fiske, 1989; Willis, 1990). This process can be seen as involving a sort of "grounded aesthetics," a process in which "meanings are attributed to symbols and practices and where symbols and practices are selected, reselected, highlighted and recomposed to resonate further appropriated and particularized meanings" (Willis, 1990, p. 21).

It is increasingly believed that the ideological support once found in critical theory for the abandonment of commercial culture is gradually dissolving. Instead, there is a growing awareness of how the culture industry not only commercially exploits the cultural needs of the youth but also provides the symbolic means that allows the young to partake in a creative appropriation of these commercial symbols. In this creative symbolic activity, people use whatever symbolic resources available that are seen as relevant to their own lives. Popular music plays an important role in contributing to the pool of symbolic resources used in this necessary symbolic work. From an ethnographic perspective, it is clearly evident that people do not passively consume symbols but actively choose from and construct their own identities from available symbolic materials. We should not forget, however, that part of music's meaning is based on its institutional nature, bound to a specific historic situation, in the context of listening that is independent of and yet part of our musical competence.

Since the 1980s, the trend in cultural studies has been to turn to so-called everyday life experiences instead of studying the extraordinary or heroic moments in life. Featherstone (1992) outlined some of the main characteristics of everyday life, among which are

- An emphasis upon what happens every day, the routine, repetitive, taken for granted experiences, beliefs, and practices; the mundane ordinary world, untouched by great events and the extraordinary
- The sphere of reproduction and maintenance
- An emphasis upon the present, which provides a nonreflexive sense of immersion in the immediacy of current experiences and activities
- A focus on the non-individual embodied sense of being together in spontaneous common activities outside of the institutional domains; an emphasis upon common sensuality, being with others in frivolous, playful sociability
- An emphasis upon heterogeneous knowledge (pp. 160ff)

There is a striking difference when we contrast this concept of "everyday life" with research on the psychology of music. Most such research purporting to say something about musical experience has been oriented toward the extraordinary, the "peak experience." Such research has traditionally used classical music—that is, music in the classical romantic tradition—as its music paradigm. In reports on this research, there is often the assumption that music takes us into an extraterrestrial territory, somewhere above ordinary life, or into some inner reality more real or authentic than what we experience in the everyday. I do not argue or question the validity of all the reports describing the adventures of people who experience this transcendental reality, something important in identity building. We should note, however, that this research is built on a kind of metaphysical assumption that there are such realities and that this research is discourse that creates this idealistic concept of humankind. Of course, this research's findings also confirm that music can carry people away to other realities or make possible these discourses. It is probably important to consider the fact that music creates a very strong illusion of naturalness because of its strong emotional effect; it is a catalyst for emotions. If this is the case, then we must investigate the ideological role of emotion in the discourse that aims to create a specific "naturalized" concept of subjectivity.

MUSIC AS A
SOUNDTRACK FOR LIFE

Consider the following hypothesis: All music in society and in media create a system of symbols that draw a map of modern realities or life forms. To appropriate this system of symbols means to internalize a map of history and contemporary culture. To be musical, then—or, more correctly, to be socialized into a specific musical competence—is to master a cognitive system in which sound represents memories, associations, histories, and traces of situations in which other people's subjectivities and experienced realities are represented through sounds. Music is not "regular vibrations," as we were told in school by our natural-science teachers. It is a system of signs, a cultural organization of sounds we have to assimilate in order to contain meaning, a meaning tied to the perception of a dual code: of the internal play of signs in music and of the references that link sound to social and cultural entities or to private life worlds.

All the kinds of music surrounding us may be seen as flexible maps of modern life worlds. These maps can change when contexts change. Each sound carries traces of a history, a small narrative from a local scene. The idea that music functions as a map that helps organize a sense of identity may be compared to the soundtrack of a fully scored film. It may help structure our autobiography by punctuating and binding together significant life events. It may contain leitmotifs that signal broader cultural formations and ideologies, personal character, values, and lifestyles. As a well-functioning soundtrack, it locates incidents in time and space and adds depths and dimensions of inner space to life events. Just as a soundtrack gives credibility to a cinematic story, our music may even make us believe that identity is natural, not constructed and negotiated through a series of choices.

Thus, music can no longer be conceived of as an universal language, something common in content and meaning despite cultural differences. We ought to be suspicious of all attempts to generalize the aesthetics of music. Such attempts to make our private subcultural musical theories general too often lead to attempts at cultural cleansing, or worse, to attempts to cleanse the "lower" art forms from "culture." If I were pessimistic, I would say that nowhere in culture is there such a temptation to become a cultural racist as there is in the field of music. A little cultural hygienic lives in each of us. The passion of the discourse about music bolsters the suspicion that our own musical and cultural experiences of truth, beauty, and morality make it hard for us to believe that others have the right to experience their own—perhaps even an opposite—musical or cultural reality.

There is always a danger that when musicologists discover that other researchers recognize the importance of music, they become both egocentric and obsessive about the role of music among other systems of symbols or art worlds. Music is only one among many systems of symbols that play an important part in young people's lives or in society in general. It might even be that the role of music for certain groups—for instance, among girls—is downplayed in relation to films, fashion, literature, and so on. A good deal of popular music research has centered on the young male guitar player, excluding girls or other forms of popular music.

It could be argued, however, that there is a special relationship between music and emotion, at least in Western culture, and that this discursive use of music as a metaphor for emotional expression gives music a special place among art forms. The study of music may thus methodologically give access to the dynamics of "symbolic work" in the domain of emotional arousal.

MUSIC AS AN ORGANIZER
OF SOCIAL LIFE

Let us now return to the actual empirical study to discuss some of our findings. The band in question, Sunwheels, was initiated in 1977 in the basement of an apartment complex in a suburb of Oslo. Consisting of mostly medium-height concrete buildings, this suburb was similar to what can be found in other cities around the world. Four 12-years-olds were inspired by their school music teacher to form a band. Rock music was the musical cultural form they used to articulate how they felt growing up in the suburbs.

It seems reasonable to suppose, as Odd Are Berkaak (1992) argued, that these young boys, just like many other kids around the world growing up at the same time in the same kind of environment

> had to oppose and deconstruct the ideology of modernism and corporate authority coded into the physical environment by its total penetration of government institutions and the city council. The hegemonic world view of high modernity was "inscribed" in the walls of the buildings and the minds of the parents and was ridiculed, inverted, contrasted, ironized, damned and subverted in every conceivable way. Rock and roll was an idiom well suited for such ideological renovation of the *Wasteland* (p. 204).

Rock music thus became the universe of signs that created a space in which to articulate how they felt about growing up, going to school, and interacting with youth club leaders and society in general. To articulate themselves, however, they felt they had to develop a language they could trust, a language through which they could honestly express themselves. Through rock music, they could be spontaneous and immediate, which guaranteed emotional honesty and made it possible to humanize and control their environment. As they worked out and elaborated on this musical language, however, in a process that cultivated the central focusing symbols of rock music— distorted sounds and high volume—they were also initiating a process that was threatened by the music industry. That is, the music industry commercialized and falsified this language, in their experience. Rock became the place where their relationship with important current issues, such as commercialism, authority, technology, and gender, could be negotiated. Our main focus, then, was to investigate how they saw the world and how such a local ethos was attached to musical style and genre. In general terms, the project was to make concrete how musical style could be read as a process of experience (Berkaak, 1989, p. 434).

Suggesting this connection between a person's musical expression and his or her personal experiences means claiming, for example, that playing in a rock group can be seen as a way of identity-building. In other words, it is a way of constructing one's own life. An important force in this process seems to be the overwhelming feeling that young people sometimes experience: that authorities, school, teachers, society as a whole, and cultural tradition have nothing to offer them in terms of identification and meaning. The rules of performance and whole arrays of categories of experience presented by society do not seem to be in accordance with how they experience life. When the young feel marginalized, as we know from therapy, they are faced with a life-threatening situation: they find no meaning in life; there is "nowhere to run." As therapists, we often recognize this as a private or personal problem. When it is seen in the larger cultural context, we find that this feeling of dissatisfaction with life and society has been expressed in many music cultural movements from the 1950s onward. Music therapists may choose, then, to work through a medium or a particular genre charged with cultural as well as personal overtones.

After the band was formed, it quickly moved from the basement of the apartment complex to the basement of the local youth club. This meant that the group got not only a place to practice but also a scene and an audience, two necessary ingredients for practicing and mastering live music performance, which is essential to the survival of a local rock group. With the support of parents, teachers, and youth workers, the group soon became one of the main rock attractions in the local community. The very installment of the group in the youth club led to the establishment of an informal music school where, over the years, hundreds of young people obtained their musical training from their peers through the exchange of skills, instruments, and technologies.

Talking to the group and reading the local newspaper showed how the group and their performance history became part of the suburb's culture and politics. In addition to playing gigs for the youth clubs in the district, the group also performed at local political meetings against unemployment and took part in antidrug campaigns. Some of the group's songs dealing with the dangers of drug abuse became local hits.

Cultural sociologists have often said rock is a counterculture that reinforces breach and opposition ("resistance through rituals"), whereas anthropologists look at it as part of folk culture through which traditional and local community values are maintained (Frith, 1992). In our study, we witnessed both such tendencies. The group was supported by the school, their parents, and the youth club, yet the boys felt they could use a certain aesthetics of sound in the process of emancipation to create their own position among the institutions of cultural power.

I will not go into detail about all aspects of the study because what is most important to music therapists is to see how a local rock group can help socialize people into their communities while allowing the band members to maintain and develop their individuality. This finding is an important reminder that music therapy can benefit from drawing on resources in the local music community and, as I emphasized in Chapter 4, that music is a community-builder.

Lately, the process of musical socialization in various urban music cultures has been studied from the perspective of anthropological theory, showing that popular music is a significant part of socialization as well as an important contribution to social life in general (see Berkaak, 1989; Cohen, 1991; Finnegan, 1989). Through participation in musical groups, not only do people experience a sense of belonging but the existence of countless music or symbolic communities gives coherence to urban life, maintaining participants' feeling of orientation and control in life. In Finnegan's words, music is a "pathway to urban living."

Music may be seen as another raw material of social life: it is sound material transformed into symbols. In this transformation, participants in musical activities organize networks of people that are in turn linked to larger conglomerates called communities or societies. In other words, social organization around aesthetic activities shows that communities are not necessarily built by people sharing the same house, work, socioeconomic background, or neighborhood. In the modern urban environment, people partake in aesthetic communities, or "meaning-based" communities. Such communities may be concretely based on actual participation in the same suburban space, or they may be imagined communities, as when people from different rock communities all over a city attend the same clubs or concerts.

In our study, we could clearly see how the protagonists extended their social contacts from family, friends, and teachers to other neighboring rock communities and audiences, then on and on until they became a district act. Through participation in local and national rock contests, they formed broader social bonds. As the group dissolved and re-formed, steadily aiming at national and international recognition, this network found a significant polarization between the local and the international or global. In other words, to play in a rock group can be an exercise in international or global positioning. In the case of the particular band we studied, this seemed to have led to an increased awareness of the importance of the local identity. Thus, the main protagonists in our study could be characterized by a strong patriotic feeling toward the suburban milieu from which they came.

In one episodes from the band's history, the guitar player recalled an incident when he brought his amplifier out on the balcony of the third floor of his apartment building and gave a 30-minute concert for all the neighbors in the houses surrounding the football court in front. This immediately gave the band an annoying presence in the local community, thus giving him, the band, and their local fans a cultural platform or position. In a sense, we can say that their high-volume distorted sound was inscribed into a particular geographical space, transforming it into a personal cultural space. This space was encoded in the hard-rock sound, which added an important dimension to the signification history of the sound for this particular interpretative community.

Our study also demonstrated how the musicians built and signaled their identities, values, and ideologies by choosing symbols from the large pool of rock symbols. Although all the band members belonged to the same hard-rock tradition, sounds and technologies sufficiently different were available from which to build and mark strong, divergent personalities and ideological profiles within the band. At the one end, we found the guitar player expressing a traditional romantic attitude based on the values of spontaneous emotion and of drawing from personal, inherent musical abilities. This attitude seems to be quite common in rock culture; in this tradition, the natural is depicted as synonymous with the uncorrupted, pure, and honest. (For a discussion of the politics of emotion, see Abu-Lughod and Lutz, 1990; Berkaak, 1989; Lutz, 1988; and Ruud, 1991.) This set of values, of course, gives great strength and credibility to the performer, seen from the fan's perspective. Other band members emphasized traditional working-class values, giving great merit to work, stability, and responsibility. Sometimes this system of values translated into excessive music practice. For others, the band became a place to exercise control, leadership, creativity, and musical excellence. Yet others saw rock as a way to realize a more hedonistic lifestyle, as is often witnessed in the images of leading commercial rock groups. We also saw that the rock group—and later, the rock community—was a place in which to gain the contacts and skills—the platform—necessary to start a career in the rock business, with its liberal economic values. (For details, see Berkaak and Ruud, 1990). All this negates theories claiming the conformity of the popular-music audience.

In other words, rock music is a scene in which individual values may be fulfilled to a large extent. This leads to a organizational problem for most groups: the tension created as a result of various musical choices will sooner or later lead to the dissolution of the rock group. In our study, we witnessed the group, in collective compositional practice, arguing at length about musical details. In the studio, we saw how band members' divergent sonorous aesthetic ideals were negotiated not only internally but with the ideals of the producer, the publishing company, or the imagined audience. This process made it clear that every commercial rock product is the end result of a series of negotiations involving a large number of people.

Thus, the accusation that rock music has been commercialized, an argument often used, by those who see themselves as representing high art, against popular music, is not necessarily a relevant to local rock musicians. There is a highly developed critical awareness among rock musicians themselves about the commercial context in which they operate. Also, because of the nature of the creative process, we must make a distinction between the musical processes and the economic exploitation of these local creative processes by the music industry. The general claim of the commercial nature of popular music is more a statement about the rock business than about rock musicians and their local practice.

An awareness of the personal ideologies are involved in the choice and appropriation of musical symbols will of course be of value to music therapists. In addition, these findings also have implications for how we perceive the whole issue of musical communication, the study of sending and receiving musical symbols, and the whole cultural debate about influences or effects.

Our interviews with local musicians also pointed to the centrality of the personal music aesthetics developed in interaction with rock music. We found that hard rock set up a groove indicative of the group's aesthetic standard. Through years of practice, the members developed a sensitivity to timing or deviance from the basic beat, which has been termed "participatory discrepancies" (Keil, 1966, 1987; Keil and Feld, 1994). Musicians gain great pleasure from exercising and experiencing the right "groove," just as getting into the groove becomes a mark of intense communication and the perceived naturalness of musical symbols. (Compare Feld's study [1988] of the "iconicity" of music among the Kaluli.) We saw that maintaining the groove was especially important in a later phase of the band: when members were introduced to and used new musical technology (synthesizer, drum machines, sampling equipment, multitrack audio recording equipment, computer-based sequence programs), maintenance of the right groove came to indicate mastery of and humanizing of technology. This has implications for our understanding of the relationship of human beings to technology in general and of how popular music provides the symbolic means to mediate the symbolic work necessary for coming to terms with new technologies. In summary, it can be said that local aesthetics establish a personal space and help produce a rich personal source of meaning and of belonging to a cultural period or a local community; that is, they help position people within a complex contemporary society.

Chapter 7

IMPROVISATION, INTERPRETATION, AND QUALITATIVE RESEARCH

There are some implicit notions in music therapy research, one of which concerns methodology. It is often derived from positivistic or natural-science procedures. Research in our field has often come to mean the measurement or evaluation of the effects of music as a therapeutic means. As explained in Chapter 1, this clinical-positivistic turn is understandable from a historical perspective: music therapy, as a young paramedical field, sought recognition by the larger academic and scientific community.

Such standards are subject to change, however, as are the areas studied. Today, music therapy needs a broad base of research, ranging from the clinical-positivistic (via case studies), to interpretative clinical research, to sociological-historical research, to philosophical-conceptual research into the nature of music. In some traditions, the emphasis on the clinical and measurable effects of music has led to a neglect of questions about the aesthetics—or the rhetoric—of music. In this chapter, I will argue that interpretation and qualitative research methods in particular are basic to improvisational music therapy.

THE NEED FOR INTERPRETATION

In his essay "Thick Description: Toward an Interpretative Theory of Culture," Clifford Geertz (1973) borrowed an example from the philosopher Gilbert Ryle:

> Consider, he (Ryle) says, two boys rapidly contracting the eyelids of their right eyes. In one, this is an involuntary twitch; in the other, a conspiratory signal to a friend. The two

movements are, as movements, identical; from an I-am-a-camera, "phenomenalistic" observation of them alone, one could not tell which was twitch and which was wink, or indeed whether both or either was twitch or wink. Yet the difference, however unphotographable, between a twitch and a wink is vast, as anyone unfortunate enough to have had the first taken for the second knows. The winker is communicating, and indeed communicating in a quite precise and special way: (1) deliberately, (2) to someone in particular, (3) to impart a particular message, (4) according to a socially established code, and (5) without cognizance of the rest of the company. . . . Suppose . . . there is a third boy, who, "to give malicious amusement to his cronies," parodies the first boy's wink, as amateurish, clumsy, obvious, and so on. He, of course, does this in the same way the second boy winked and the first twitched: by contracting his right eyelid (pp. 6–7).

Geertz elaborates on this example, showing multiple possible situations and intentions behind "blinking behavior." For music therapists facing the live or taped improvisational situation, the dilemma may seem familiar: how do we decide what the client's actual intention is? When do we know when the client is merely imitating us, expressing herself "authentically," or pretending to go along with the rules of the game we set?

The example above convincingly demonstrates the limitations of a research method based on mere recording, observing, and registering the client's behavior. For therapists who work in a hermeneutic tradition and apply either humanistic or analytic methods, the need to develop procedures to help "read" the client's improvisation seems obvious. These should be of such quality, however, that we can call them research procedures.

What is the nature of qualitative research? What is the difference between quantitative and qualitative methods, and how can qualitative research qualify as science?

We might say that the application of qualitative methods is concerned with the understanding of psychic qualities. Because qualitative methods focus on the concrete and unique in a process and are directed at the experience, they are appropriate in music therapy when the intention is to interpret and understand the meaning of an improvisation to understand the client's special mode of expression. These methods will satisfy a demand for immediacy and closeness in the comprehension of the single treatment or improvisational process. This suggests that it is important to hold on to the first prescientific and immediate understanding but also to try to contain such experiences within scientific expression.

The criteria of reproduction, of significance in the natural sciences, is replaced in qualitative research by the criteria of documentation. Any statement about a musical process should be documented with tapes or a transcription. As it is impossible to repeat an improvisation (which in itself excludes a certain form of scientific reproduction), qualitative research must document the sound context behind the interpretation or the chain of arguments. This is important particularly because music may be verbally restated or represented in different ways according to the theoretical model chosen, as we saw in Chapter 5. We must demand from such a method step-by-step documentation of its process of interpretation.

Charging that qualitative research is not without any presuppositions does not, however, make any sense. The qualitative paradigm carries an implicit understanding that our values or theoretical presuppositions determine how we perceive "facts." This charge, then, might as well be raised against natural-science procedures, too, because it is a general scientific or epistemological problem.

A particular characteristic of qualitative methods is the search for meaning and significance in psychological phenomena. It is a basic presupposition that psychic processes refer to a context of meaning that can be studied as manifested in the music or client–therapist interaction. A problem arises, however, in explaining context. Is meaning to be found and studied in the psychic phenomena itself, or does it come out of or is it produced by the social interaction? The latter view, which is more ethnographic, may have methodological consequences, although it does not necessarily disqualify the applicability of qualitative methods.

Also implied in the qualitative approach is the notion that the method chosen should fit the phenomenon under scrutiny. If we want to trace the meaning of psychic processes, we need a certain flexibility or mobility in our methods. Following the movements of the phenomenon requires a co-movement: the ability to be moved is an important part of the method itself. Thus, we see that ideals governing the qualitative method differ from those of natural science. Here, the researcher, understood as the uninfluenced, objective figure behind the instruments, passively registers what happens in the outer world (Tüpker, 1988, 1990).

Removing these standards of objectivity, however, does not mean that qualitative researchers are not concerned about results. The cue is "controlled subjectivity," which means that the researcher's subjectivity is a necessary presupposition for psychological research. The observer must be trained to keep disturbing influences at a minimum, and observations must be recorded stepwise, according to the rules of the theoretical system. Rosemarie Tüpker (1988, 1990), a German music therapist, wrote that applying this special form of participant observation, using controlled subjectivity, to the study of musical processes may have certain advantages. For example, music, when seen as the production of psychic modes of expression, always keeps moving. Music is always a process. It fulfills itself in time and makes it possible to experience time itself. There are no other or better instruments than human beings themselves to describe the movement of music. This description is necessary to transform music into a scientific object.

This is not a simple process. The researcher may be caught in the tension between involvement and the necessary detachment, between the effort to grasp what is going on and the process of being present. Qualitative research may be further characterized by its attempt to relate to the whole, or the nature of the phenomenon. It is important to ask the nature of the music in a particular improvisation, or in general, to ask what makes change possible.

REFLEXIVITY, OR SCIENCE AS METACRITIQUE

When science no longer is concerned only with explanations, predictions, or truth, the focus shifts to dealing with the presupposition behind a certain scientific school of thought. To maintain a rational dialogue in the field of music therapy, we must make explicit our concepts of music and humankind, which underlie our theories about the therapeutic application of music.

There is a definite connection between our values, interests, and norms and how we experience reality. If we accept as fact that people define or even experience reality differently, it is a scientific attitude's primary task to define the relationships between our values and the way we perceive the world. An example from improvisational music therapy illustrates this.

One of the more celebrated case histories in our field is found in the book *Creative Music Therapy,* by Paul Nordoff and Clive Robbins (1977). The case of Edward is discussed in the text and demonstrated in the cassette published with the book.

In the first session on the tape, we hear how violently Edward protests even before he enters the music therapy room. That is, it makes sense to categorize his vocalizing as screaming or rejecting; however—and this is important—this "sonic reality" may be interpreted and categorized otherwise by different therapists coming from dissimilar therapeutic or theoretical traditions. Of course, the therapeutic actions originating from these interpretations will be diverse. Some of the many interpretations of Edward's vocalizing might be crying, defiance, attention-seeking behavior, high-frequency sounds, or communication signals. *Reflexivity* means taking into consideration not only that our categories of observation are theoretically biased but also that they determine what we hear and how we perceive or interpret those sounds, which in turn creates a basis for our choice of methods.

One of the basic tenets of the critical school of the philosophy of science is that there is a correspondence between our values and interests and how we perceive the world. The ideal of a value-free science has been criticized by the hermeneutically inspired tradition. In the early days of music therapy, objectivity was held as one of the basic conditions of a scientific approach. That is, to be able to claim a scientific status for our results, we must reduce possible sources of error. To be systematically open to critique in advance, we must try to reduce some of the most characteristic sources of errors. There are, however, different types of errors. Our observations and theories may be influenced by our personalities; our cultural, social, and political backgrounds; or the particular scientific tradition to which we belong. Objectivity addresses the possibility of dealing with such sources of errors, and science has developed procedures and methods to secure objective access to the phenomena we study. This type of "objectivity" we call "intersubjectivity"; it should ensure that all researchers reach the same results when they apply the same methods of study.

Presupposition in general, however, cannot be handled by intersubjectivity. Individual researchers will always be informed by various interests or values that will influence their research activity. This preunderstanding concerns not only what we actually see and describe as researchers but also what we look for. In the example of Edward, how we perceived his sounds depended on the categories available to us or that we chose to use. His sounds could have been perceived as a "scream," as "inappropriate behavior," as a "signal," or as a "possibility for communication." This example demonstrates how different people bring to the situation a unique set of values and interests attached to the use of different categories. As professional improvisational music therapists, we are trained to perceive sounds as possible signals of communication. In a certain music therapy paradigm, music therapists are interested in maintaining such signals to develop a pattern of interaction and expression.

We can trace value systems originating from particular concepts of humankind and music. A music therapist from the humanistic tradition, for instance, may regard human beings as active and in search of meaning and music as a language, system of symbols, nonverbal system of expression, or a communication system. A scientific positivist would insist on the necessity of separating values and interests from the description of phenomena and, ideally, on value neutrality. A positivist music therapy researcher, however, would be forced to make some kind of categorization. Sometimes terms from physics would be used to describe Edward's sound—frequency, timbre, duration, and so forth. The questions are whether such terms are more neutral than those in other category systems and whether we really come closer to reality by using metaphors from physics rather than from other areas of life.

My point here is that there is a certain connection between perception and knowledge, and norms, values, interests, and actions. In other words, there is a connection between interests and perception in the sense that our values and interests inform and govern our way of perceiving the world. If we translate "action" into "music therapeutic methods," we can draw a triangle to illustrate the connection between these concepts:

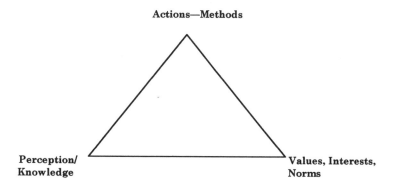

(After Jacobsen et al., 1979)

The term *norm* refers to the rules regulating perception and action. With Edward, the music therapist might have applied such rules as "Use all the sounds the child makes as a point of departure for communication and interaction" and "Try to develop the child's sounds within a communicative context." Our values are attached to certain concepts—here, a concept of music. They also inform us why this concept of music or why definite actions based on this concept may benefit the child. Part of our training and competence is mastering different arguments for the possible beneficial influence of music. In other words, we act from a belief in the value of the type of activities we want to initiate. When the term *interests* is used here, it is because we must always ask who may benefit from the action. Music therapists may argue that it is in the child's interest to develop a repertoire of sounds to be used in a communication context.

We may imagine, however, that behind other ways of categorizing the child's sounds—for instance, as "screams and noise"— we would find more short-term interests concerning creating an endurable work situation for the staff. It is not moralistic to say that such factors as wages, work conditions, and number of staff influence which systems of categorization are used. Again, this has to do with how society sets its priorities.

What I want to make explicit is that there is a definite connection between interests and perception/knowledge and that this connection may be colored by society's prevailing ideas and attitudes. In this framework, the question arises of whose interests govern a music therapist's work. It may be that the values of music therapists as a professional group inform the work of a particular therapist. We should ask whether a particular therapeutic tactic is really in the client's interest or is instead informed by society's interest in making sure everyone fits a limited concept of normality. In other words, we must always be critical of our own practices to determine if it is really in the interest of our clients to develop certain competencies.

QUALITATIVE METHODS

As I mentioned earlier, anyone investigating music therapy improvisations, as with Edward, for instance, would encounter many difficulties using positivist scientific procedures. In the 1980s, we saw the emergence of a qualitative research approach in music therapy that we might argue better captures the uniqueness of the improvisational method. The main characteristics of the qualitative approach are as follows:

1. *Qualitative research is holistic.* Research is organized around an entire case, group, or classroom, with the purpose of understanding particular incidents. Its focus may be on the person, the experiences of people involved, events, or materials (Aldridge, 1994; Bruscia, 1995b). Thus, it seems reasonable that a particular improvisation (or several) could serve as a possible focus for study.
2. *Qualitative research is empirical and naturalistic.* Research takes place in the natural setting—that is, where music therapy is actually taking place—because it is the direct source for gathering data.
3. *Qualitative research is descriptive.* Sounds/music, words, and pictures, rather than numbers, are the focus. Interpretation starts with information contained in the situation and includes experiences or transcripts of music, transcripts of interviews, field notes, videotapes, audiotapes, personal documents, and more. Because research involving improvisation (or clinical research in general) cannot be replicated, *documentation* is crucial. What the Germans call *Nachvollziehbarkeit*—the chain of evidence, or the ability to trace and follow any statement about the

world, description, or representation of the situation or event back to the sound, verbal statement, picture (tapes, videos, paintings), and so on—is vital to music therapy. Because there is no way to repeat an improvisation, which in itself excludes the scientific paradigm of replicability, we must document the sound behind the interpretation, especially dealing with music. This is because of the polysemous quality of music, the innumerable ways music may be represented through verbal metaphors.

4. *Qualitative research is interpretative.* A basic condition for our interaction with the world is that we build our concepts and understanding on our interpretation of the information our senses provide. Thus, the basic scientific tool must be hermeneutics, or the science of interpretation.

5. *Qualitative research is emphatic.* Research must focus on the intentions of the participants we observe. If our purpose is to grasp the concrete and immediate meaning of an improvisation or to understand what lies behind a certain manner of expression, qualitative research seems to be the best method. Qualitative researchers differ, however, in their views of the meaning of music. Some may look into the structure of the material/event to study a sort of "embodied" meaning. Others may adopt the relativistic attitude of anthropologists to study how people construct meaning in a particular context.

6. *Qualitative research is sometimes based on grounded theory.* Data is analyzed inductively, or from what is called a "bottom-up" perspective.

7. *Qualitative research emphasizes immediate observations and spontaneous interpretations.* As Tüpker (1990) argued, this emphasis satisfies the need for closeness to facilitate understanding the improvisation in question. This also provides the necessary flexibility—the ability to let ourselves be moved by the situation, the music. Instead of trying to live up to the positivistic ideal of the neutral, objective researcher, qualitative methods take advantage of the participating researcher who stands in a particular relation to the phenomena under study. That this method acknowledges subjectivity, of course, raises

serious questions of validity. Tüpker called for "controlled subjectivity," which involves the ability to avoid distracting or harmful influences. Other qualitative researchers emphasize various methods of triangulation.

In emphasizing controlled subjectivity, we do not lose our primarily prescientific and immediate understanding; we do try to explain such experiences with scientific statements. This is especially important if we want to contain the bodily expression that is often behind the musical gesture. In Edmund Husserl's terminology, the interpretation's spontaneity is an attempt to ensure that we capture the bodily *Fundierung* in the verbal representation (Widdershoven, 1993). Such an interpretative perspective, in which the "nature" of the phenomena is explicit and related to the interpreter's preunderstanding, may well suit the demands of reflexivity and metacriticism, discussed earlier.

Generally, it could be said that music therapy, as a human or interpretative science, is mainly interested in the investigation of the relationships between the musical signs originating in the transactions between client and therapist and those changes in the client's experience or behavior that stem from the processes of signification within or between client and therapist as a result of their musical interaction. This would imply the necessity of developing some tools of interpretation for reading the interplay among musical structures, the client's experiences, and the therapist's interventions. One possible strategy for deconstructing this triadic process would be to postulate that the whole music therapy situation is a "text." Then we could benefit from the theoretical and methodological diversity of human sciences: literary and cultural studies, narrative analysis, rhetoric, semiotics, discourse theory, and structural analysis, for example.

COMPETING CLAIMS OF KNOWLEDGE

Two of the underlying assumptions of qualitative research in music therapy are that the aim is not to reach some kind of truth, in the sense of describing a single reality, and that using a particular method does not guarantee that the results can be compared with some preset standard of truth. As Ken Aigen said in his opening address at the First Symposium on Qualitative Research in Music Therapy in Düsseldorf in July 1994, "Method is neither a guarantor nor an arbiter of truth. Because so much of qualitative research is dependent upon the skills, personal qualities, and insight of the researcher, it is possible that a given method could be meticulously followed and still not produce valuable or trustworthy findings" (Aigen, 1994, p. 11; for more information about the papers read at the symposium, see Langenberg et al., 1996). Instead, qualitative research acknowledges that multiple realities exist, or, as Ken Bruscia stated, "that truth and reality exist in the form of multiple, intangible mental constructions" (Bruscia, 1994, p. 6). The best we can achieve is a better understanding of the particular reality we are involved in or share in some areas with a particular client. Does this mean that qualitative research is not concerned with possible competing claims of knowledge? How are various aspects of "validity" dealt with?

Some approaches live up to this ideal of relative truth and try to obtain some kind of validity in the traditional sense. For instance, although Henk Smeijsters recognizes the importance of qualitative research designs, he reminds us that it is important not to give up "the accepted criteria for sound scientific research." He argues that we need criteria for validity; thus, he sees the problem of validity as a methodological one (Smeijsters, 1994, p. 1) to be solved in an empirical or positivist epistemology. We might ask, however, if the problem of conflicting claims of knowledge is a methodological one or if it belongs instead to the epistemological domain. If the latter is the case, we must deal with different epistemologies pertaining to various methodological approaches. It is not, then, a question of taking traditional methodological precautions to achieve validity. (For additional commentary on this problem, see Smeijsters, 1997.)

In the positivist paradigm, we find a concept of truth in which the data are looked upon as corresponding with reality. This is called the correspondence theory of truth. By contrast, qualitative research considers data to be "constructed" in some way. Because there is no way to know the reality directly but only through language and perception, the qualitative (or hermeneutic) effort aims to reveal some kind of meaning or significance in the data. This is in accordance with a broader interpretative background, the hermeneutic concept of truth, or what is sometimes called the coherence theory of truth. The coherence criterion refers to the unity, consistency, and internal logic of a statement (see Kvale, 1989). Thus qualitative researchers, when

they talk about accuracy, mean "appropriate (metaphoric) representation," not "correspondence."

There is a third concept of truth prevailing in the contemporary
theory of science—the pragmatic point of view, concerned with measuring "truth" against its practical consequences, its usefulness (see
Alvesson and Sköldberg, 1994).

The triangle below represents the various paradigms dominating different schools of research in music therapy today.

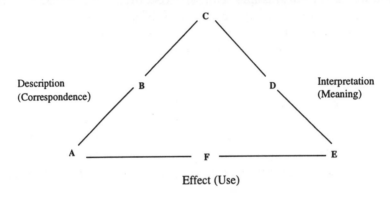

Let us first look at the traditional view of science. If our research is
wholly identified as "outcome research," we can apply a pragmatic
criterion to evaluate whether the knowledge we produce is "true."
This position is point F in our model. Behavioral studies, for instance,
are concerned with the "contingent use of music"—with its effect on
behavior, not its meaning for the patient.

The problem with such a position is that it tells us nothing
about the processes leading to change in behavior; it tells us nothing
about music as an important facilitator in the process. If we move left
in our model, we find researcher A, who not only will try to account
for changes in the client's behavior but will also create an operational
definition of the music used or the behavior involved. This is often
done within the paradigm of empirical epistemology by using concepts from physics or acoustics to obtain "correct" data or intersub-
jectively shared statements. Therapist A, then, finds himself in a
descriptive-pragmatic mode in which the significance of music is
downplayed and descriptions (of music or behavior) are close to data.
This is also a technique in which theory-building has less importance

than theory corroboration and verification. (In this sense, the former *Journal of Music Therapy* was the most well-known chronicle of the music therapy verification proletariat.)

Position *B* is assumed by the positivist researcher most concerned with describing the data. In research focusing on analysis of the music, this leads to a detailed description of the musical parameters according to some system of analysis. In some of these systems, analysis often starts from this level, either close to the score, transcription, or phenomenological experience. Some close readings of the music of phenomenologists would belong in the area between points *B* and *C*, depending on the recognition of their own preunderstanding (Husserl versus Martin Heidegger). It is interesting to see how close phenomenology comes to the positivistic standard of truth when it insists on describing the "essence" of a phenomenon, a so-called naive realism. On the other hand, phenomenologists recognize the inner relationship between our perception of the world and our preunderstanding. A crucial point is that this implies that a constructed reality must be substituted for a naive realism.

Analyst *C* would try to take the stance that the investigation of the phenomenon reveals its nature by saying something about its significance. Although this position does not fully recognize this meaning as a construct or fully focus on finding a deeper cultural or biographical meaning, analysis from this vantage point tends to stay close to the structure of music or the supposed "natural categories" that evolve from close investigation of the client's experiences.

Position *D*, however, removes itself from the idea that it is possible to describe the music or the patient's experience "as they are," or as the client's "true experience." From the hermeneutic interpretation, there is always a deeper underlying theme, a significance that can only be *interpreted*. We can clearly see this in Dorit Amir's writing: "I wanted to find out more about the meaning of the experience of music therapy for those who are involved as therapists and clients" (Amir, 1994, p. 2). Although Amir explicitly described the process leading to her categories, we could posit that they are constructed to some extent. Amir seems faithful to the orthodox tenets of grounded theory, focusing on the empirical nature of her categories. This empirical turn is supported by her list of credibility measures: intensive contact with subjects, triangulation, peer debriefing, negative case analysis, and member checks. Her hermeneutic approach to the "meaning behind" events is influenced by empirical epistemology.

There seems to be less today of the postmodern approach to qualitative research. One exception may be Carolyn Kenny (1994), whose paper at the Düsseldorf Symposium brought narrative, critical theory, and a deconstructive attitude to the question of methodology. Only the future can tell if one day even music therapy researchers find the text (music, experience) irrelevant as an "authentic expression" that informs us about the client's "inner life," taking the text into consideration only as being produced in the context of other texts. That is, improvised music, for instance, is understood not with reference to some underlying musical structure or to the client's biography but to the musical code developed in previous sessions.

Moving toward point E in our paradigm representation would allow the narrative and rhetorical character of our knowledge to also be used in the important task of theory-building. We would have the necessary feedback from the larger intersubjective community of therapists about the reality of our thoughts and actions.

SCIENCE AS NARRATIVE

It seems that my route through the field of music therapy has led me to the interpretative paradigm. I have learned from the community of music therapists how differently each has come to perceive reality and the nature of his or her work differently. I have learned that their outlook on life and their values and interests color their way of looking at the process of research, their way of pursuing a truth. As I have argued, however, there is no single truth, no single reality. Our profession will forever be populated with people and paradigms with competing claims of knowledge. The only answer is to learn from each other and communicate what we learn.

Since the 1980s, our field has undergone a general shift of view regarding what is scientific: from measurement to interpretation, from quantitative to qualitative, from mechanistic and organismic thinking to the more narrative and discursive. Music therapy now seeks recognition from natural-science models; a hermeneutic approach, as in analytic therapy; or a more phenomenological approach, as sometimes seen in the humanistic tradition. The three main research approaches today in our field are as follows:

- The behavioral version of the natural-science model is a pragmatic approach that seeks to establish truth value by measuring the effects of music in therapy.
- The hermeneutic tradition focuses its efforts on meaning, trying to reveal some of the hidden layers of meaning behind the client's behavior while involved in symbolic interaction with music.
- The phenomenological approach seeks truth by revealing the essence of what music "really is," defining the core or nature of music or musical behavior observed in the clinical situation.

These approaches all have strengths and weaknesses when scrutinized from the philosophy of science. The natural-science approach, when closely attached to a positivistic system of values, has been criticized because of its beliefs in objective, "pure" data, as if it were possible to describe something without considering values and ideas. The behavioral music therapist following this positivistic model is of course selecting and interpreting what is important to focus on, disregarding phenomena that are important from another theoretical perspective. The phenomenological researcher may also be criticized for sometimes making naive assumptions about the possibility of defining essences, of seeing things "as they really are," as if the world could be defined without a language code and outside a cultural context. The historical character of language, as it has been transformed and infused by ideologies and cultural values, may make any effort to define the essence of something no more than a good representation, a good story. This problem can be addressed by establishing a broader interpretative approach, as in some hermeneutic traditions, where truth is sought not as a possible correspondence between reality and the phenomena observed but as one between the phenomena and a broader interpretative context. Often, however, hermeneutic interpretation has been exercised too subjectively, as if the researcher has some kind of superperspective on reality (or the client–music situation), an ability to speak for us all, regardless of cultural position.

I am not saying any of these three positions is illegitimate. In a postmodern climate, there is room for many values and approaches. Music therapy certainly needs the pragmatic evaluation of the effects of music in therapy, good essential descriptions of musical behavior, and a broader contextual interpretation of our symbolic interaction with music. There is no easy way out; no way to see the world as a single reality; no way to reach truth through better measurements, more exact definitions, or deeper interpretations. Instead I plead that music therapists accept the discursive and narrative aspects of their scientific activities. What does this mean?

First, if we accept the idea that we live in different subjective realities, informed by different languages, values, and cultural realities, there can be no general objective theories in music therapy. This means it is impossible to make statements about music therapy or music that are generalizable to all client populations or methodological approaches. Truth is local, and the best we can do is make good interpretations and write good descriptions of what happened there and then. Second, our interpretations and descriptions are always communicated through language. This means our descriptions of reality are forced into our choice of metaphors and narrative structure. However we see music, whether as "communication," "interaction," "reinforcement," "expression," or something else, we choose our metaphors from other fields of language, other theoretical models. Of course, sometimes our choice of metaphors or our ways of enacting the music therapy situation may prove rhetorically efficient, especially when our choice of narrative comes from a well-respected related discipline. Third, we should be aware that our ways of describing, interpreting, or "proving the effects of" music therapy are a kind of discourse that creates the reality we believe in—and that we want other people to believe in. In therapy, this discourse must be felt as "true," lest we encounter both grave ethical and serious practical problems in dealing with clients. Fourth, scientific activity means a high degree of reflexivity, an aspect that may create a conflict within the music therapist as researcher and the music therapist as clinician. As researchers, we must always deal with the underlying values of our activity, our ways of conceptualizing and narrating our perceptions. This, in the end, reveals the contingency of our ways of telling the story of our work, the arbitrary nature of our choice of communicative form.

Chapter 8

IMPROVISATION
AS A LIMINAL EXPERIENCE

To improvise means to create or arrange something "here and now," to put something together as you go, from available resources. *Webster's Dictionar,* which I quote from Bruscia (1987, pp. 5–6), defines *improvisation* as "to make, invent, or arrange offhand." The Latin *improvisio* means "unforeseen." In music, *improvising* is defined as "the art of spontaneously creating music (ex tempore) while playing, rather than performing a composition already written" (*The Harvard Brief Dictionary of Music,* cited in Bruscia, 1987, pp. 5–6). Grootaers (1983, pp. 245–246) defined it as "testing, fooling around, nosing around without a plan." In everyday life (and particularly during vacations), we experience improvisation as being at the fringes of "real" life, a time during which we *prepare* ourselves for the "real" experience to come, or as something we find ourselves doing "in the meantime." Thus, journeys themselves are often situations for improvisation, when we are confronted with new people.

Improvisation has an element of prepared aimlessness. Improvisations may even be well prepared in the sense that certain elements have been previously selected, even though the order of these elements and extent to which they are to be used has not been decided. Themes may have been considered thoroughly without necessarily having been performed. The jazz musician has acquired an arsenal of musical formulas, scales, and riffs, along with "rules" that determine how such materials can be performed or recreated. A certain jazz style presupposes knowledge of musical codes and materials. A successful improvisation can occur when the musicians play either with or against musical conventions (Kruse, 1990–1991, p. 9). In music therapy, the stylistic conventions may be fewer, but there are conventions that decide which group processes, associations, or extramusical themes belong in the therapy context.

Improvisation can also be seen as creating an opportunity for change, transformation, and process to come into focus. In this sense, improvisation means to get not just from one place to another but from one *state* to another. It means to change one's *relationship* with other people, phenomena, and situations—even one's relationship with oneself. Therefore, we can see it as a transitional ritual, a way of changing position, framework, status, or states of consciousness.

The purpose of this chapter is to demonstrate how improvisation, as an important element in music therapy, may be meaningfully studied in light of anthropological theory. There are aspects common to all forms of improvisational music therapy, regardless of the therapeutic ideology on which treatment is based. Using the anthropological study tool of extended contextual understanding, I hope to provide a general understanding of the role or power of music in improvisational music therapy. I will illustrate the discussion with actual examples from jazz performances in the hope of showing that improvisation has cultural meanings beyond the pure aesthetic or artistic aspects of the music. Thus, this chapter can be read as a cultural analysis of the role of music in the everyday rituals that serve to change or maintain aspects of contemporary culture.

IMPROVISATION AS PLAY

German music therapist Frank Grootaers (1983, pp. 245–246) wrote that in music therapy, it is exactly those marginal situations in life—what he calls *Zwischenwelten* (between worlds)—that become the focus of attention. It is the spontaneous idea, the unforeseen connection of seemingly meaningless thoughts, that becomes the center of attention. It is the accidental plucking of sound sources that interests us more than logical rules, compositional precision, or artistic virtuosity. Although music therapists do not renounce musical quality, what concerns us here is the spontaneous common product that stems from the interaction between client and therapist (Bruscia, 1987, pp. 5–6). It is the poetic or aesthetic aspect of the musical communication, however, that can transform the improvisation into a therapeutic tool.

Improvisation has many similarities with play, which is defined as actions characterized by a certain way of *organizing* activities rather than by a particular set of activities. This means that play can occur as we carry out tasks that are generally characterized as work. By changing the rules, we create new frames or a new referential perspective of the situation. This level of communication, called metacommunication (Bateson, 1973a), places cognitive boundaries around certain forms of behavior and states that they are either play or ordinary life.

Anthropologists Emily Schultz and Robert Lavenda (1990, p. 158) wrote that play allows us to see that perspective in everyday life is relative and that there are other angles from which we can make sense of everyday experience. Play exists, they wrote, when there are two sets of rules and two different goals—one operating here and now and one that applies outside the given reality. Play makes us aware of alternatives and creates a space in which it is possible to choose between different actions, a situation basic to therapeutic improvisation.

This awareness creates what is referred to as the paradox of play: it is supposed to be divorced from reality, yet it is ripe with the consequences of everyday life. It is an "as if" activity, but the possibilities illustrated by play can have real consequence if the activity is taken out of the frame of play. Another anthropologist, Don Handelman (Schultz and Lavenda, 1990, p. 156), emphasized that play is reflexive: it teaches us that events can be understood in other ways when taken out of their context. Play tells us not how things *should* be but rather how things *might* be. It is of course important to the therapeutic process that improvisation creates a frame that allows expression of a variety of fantasies from different spheres of the client's life. These fantasies appear in combinations that would otherwise be intolerable for the client outside the framework of play. Musical improvisation, then, is play with musical tendencies and possibilities as a frame within which fantasies and alternative forms of action can be explored.

There is a difference in style between improvisations in music therapy and jazz improvisations. Those in music therapy have fewer musical rules and conventions to follow, and musical frames can be established by the participants while they play. This means that such improvisations can be free of the extramusical connotations often attached to a certain musical style. Music therapy improvisations are total, much like those in the avant-garde or free jazz genres. At the same time, the resulting musical material are free to function as metaphors of the different types of themes central to therapeutic improvisation. Because we handle the improvisation within the cognitive boundaries of what our culture defines as therapy, its themes are significant in the therapeutic context. It is this "therapeutic reality"—which deals with existential themes, conflicts, or dramatic life circumstances—that we seek to transform through improvisation as play.

RITES OF PASSAGE

The term *rites of passage* was first used by Belgian anthropologist Arnold Van Gennep, who at the beginning of the twentieth century observed that certain rituals around the world, associated with movement or passage from one position in a social structure to another, had similar structures. These included births, initiations, confirmations, weddings, funerals, and the like.

Van Gennep discovered that all these rituals begin with a period of separation from the old position and from normal time. During this period, the ritual passenger must leave behind the symbols and practices of his or her previous position. The second stage involves a period of transition in which the ritual passenger is in a twilight zone between the old and the new worlds, a period of ambiguity, perceived danger, and the absence of roles. The final stage is that of reaggregation, in which the ritual passenger is reintroduced into society, but this time in his or her new position.

Anthropologist Victor Turner added a great deal to our understanding of the transition period, which he referred to as the liminal period, from the Latin *limen,* or "threshold." It is characteristic of being on the threshold that one is "neither here nor there, betwixt and between" (Turner, 1974, p. 232). The symbolism of the rite of passage often expresses this ambiguous state. As I will discuss further later, people experiencing the liminal state together tend to develop an intense comradeship in which their nonliminal distinctions disappear or become irrelevant. Turner called this modality of social relationship *communitas,* or an unstructured group or community consisting of equal individuals.

Musical improvisations may be thought of as part of a wide-ranging transitional ritual—as an experience of liminality. Both rituals in general and more specific rites of passage appear within many contexts and on many levels both in the jazz world and in music therapy. For instance, there are rituals for initiating young jazz musicians into the professional jazz community. We can also look on the training of the music therapist as a long rite of passage. Within the training program itself are situations that may be studied as rites of passage: Norwegian music therapy students, for example, go on a journey to the countryside each semester (separation). Here they are exposed to a state of insecurity, a setting for self-realization. This weekend is led, for example, by a Gestalt therapist, who counsels the students before they collect themselves prior to returning home (reaggregation).

Let us turn our focus to musical improvisation. Just what it is that gives musical improvisation such a central symbolic role—a tool that can be used to enact a liminal situation—as preparation for the transition from one state to another?

LIMINALITY

Liminal states or processes are characterized by confusion, ambiguity, and the dissolution of conventional meanings and fixed points in life. Essential to the experience is the feeling of timelessness—"a moment in and out of time," as Turner wrote (1969, p. 96). Grootaers came close to a description of such liminal processes when he characterized improvisation as a possibility for experiencing "the rules of the soul." By nosing around in old matters, we may discover new meanings and at the same time *lose* ourselves in thought. This is because in improvisation, many things happen at the same time, Grootaers explained.

The same can have many meanings at the same time; meanings can change so much that they must be reinterpreted. The unambiguous becomes repressed by the ambiguous, which in turn come into focus. What may have appeared as whole or connected will suddenly appear as made up and accidental. What was previously associated with peace suddenly becomes unpleasant, Grootaers wrote (1983, pp. 246, 250). His description is reminiscent of Freud's concept of primary processes, forms of thoughts in which dimensions of time and categories of space have not yet been developed, a state in which past and future are not anchored in reality and thoughts are colored by images, simultaneity, and contrast.

For music therapist Fritz Hegi, improvisation is a field of experimentation with the content of life (or as Carolyn Kenny suggested, a field of play [Kenny, 1989]), where we can learn to transcend previously defined borders of freedom. It is an open space in which processes of listening are expanded to the extent that there is nothing that is "wrong" or without value, in which something more honest can emerge from the hidden (Hegi, 1986, p. 21).

Flow and Void

In the description of the liminal, as it appears directly in musical processes, we find two especially important categories of experience: "flow" and "void." Psychologist Mihaly Csikszentmihalyi used the term *flow* for the psychic state in which incidences follow each other in a united, organic way without our conscious participation. He wrote that we feel in control of the situation, yet we are fully absorbed by it. We forget to make a distinction between ourselves and our surroundings, between stimulus and response, between the present and the past. Consciousness and behavior become one; life is expanded and full of meaning. As jazz pianist Mose Allison put it, "That's the challenge every night; trying to work toward that spot where it's all flowing" (Leonard, 1987, p. 75).

It is as if the improvisation enchants the surroundings and creates a flow of ideas where "everything should or ought to happen." Through this act of liberation or taking meaning back to point zero, we make possible a "space without categories," a state in which something new can evolve from nothing. Trumpeter Roy Eldridge remembers how he sat down, before he entered the bandstand, to mentally work through what he was going to play:

> But when I got out there I didn't try to make the B-flat or whatever I was thinking of, because I'd go right into a *void* where there was no memory—nothing but me. I knew the chords and I knew the melody, and I never thought about

them. I'd just be in this blank space, and the music came out anyway. It wasn't always easy (Leonard, 1987, p. 73 [italics mine]).

The key word is *void*, which points directly to the space without categories, a place abandoned by meaning. The *Concise Oxford Dictionary* defines *void*, from the Latin *vacuus*, as "empty, vacant, invalid, not binding, useless, lacking, free from, empty space, render invalid, emit, quit, evacuate." The Norwegian translation of the word contains a number of the characteristics of the liminal situation we are looking for: to undo old meaning; to empty old meaning in order to create a new space, which is in turn is filled with new meanings; to clear the space for something new.

Although it can be frightening, the experience of being "betwixt and between" creates an emotional incentive to search for new meanings and new connections. As Thad Jones said:

> In such moments . . . the music finds itself at the edge of the cliff, between the known and the frightening unknown. You play for your life with your heart in your throat. The musical ideas flow freely and uninhibited directly from the unconscious without any disturbing intervention from the rational. Maybe the ideas come from a place far away. Maybe you are in touch with the creative principle or God. Anyway, you are in touch with your fellow musicians (Oversand, 1987, p. 74 [my translation]).

Though hesitant to say so, Jones suggested that the liminal empty space can be filled with a metaphysical content. He was quite certain, however, about the quality of his contact with his fellow musicians. In other words, he experienced "communitas."

Turner wrote that incidences related to the liminal are ambiguous and that their undefinable aspects can be expressed through a rich variety of symbols. Odd Are Berkaak, a Norwegian anthropologist and a colleague of mine, showed, in his analysis of rock music as a cultural form, that rock texts and music borrow their motives from and can symbolize liminal states and phenomena. Thus, rock (as well as jazz) can be taken as an attempt to create a cultural space uninvaded by the language or forms of experience prevailing in "normal society" (Berkaak, 1993).

We could argue that similarly, music therapy improvisations attempt to create a similar space—a psychic (re)dressing room—in which clients can try out alternative forms of expressions and actions. They discover musical frames in accord with their own biographical experiences and expectations.

If we look closer at descriptions people give of their improvisation experiences, we will see a number of symbols or metaphors that delineate the cognitive boundaries that give improvisation its liminal characteristics. In other words, we can study the strategies of signification we use when we introduce and give meaning to instruments, musical material, or extramusical themes.

Turner placed special emphasis on the so-called subliminal experiences that he said lead people to new cultural positions. Take, for example, dressing in rags to cultivate an understanding of poverty. Throughout history, symbols of nakedness and disclosure have been used to oppose things that are hidden or veiled. In both Western and Eastern philosophy, this polarity symbolizes the division between a "real" world and an "illusory" one: daily life is considered to be the unreal, illusory world (as in the veil of Maya found in the Vedanta philosophy of Hinduism), whereas the "true" world is thought to be accessible only in transcending our bodies, space, and time or only in a future existence after death. In modern thought, both these worlds are on earth, in space and time, filled with human beings. The false world is seen as the historical past, a world we have lost, whereas the true physical and social world exists for us here and now. Marshall Berman (1982) wrote that at this point, a new symbolism emerges. As an example, he cited clothes as symbols of civilized life:

> Clothes become an emblem of the old-illusory mode of life; nakedness comes to signify the newly discovered and experienced truth; and the act of taking off one's clothes becomes an act of spiritual liberation, of becoming real (p. 106).

Berman uses Shakespeare's King Lear as an example. After Lear has lost both his political power and his human dignity, he throws away his clothes, a gesture that appears to be his first step to full humanity because for the first time, he recognizes a connection between himself and another human being (I–Thou). This recognition gives him greater sensitivity and insight. Berman wrote that "Shakespeare is telling us that the dreadful naked reality of the 'unaccommodated man' is the point from which accommodation must be made, the only ground on which real community can grow" (Berman, 1992, p. 108).

Berkaak argues that the liminal should not be sought only in such substructural signification—that is, in activating signs referring to anticivilization, the spontaneous, or the unplanned. We also have other strategies in our quest to break out of the conventional realm and into a "fantastic reality," four of which Berkaak mentions:

- The preliminal, where identification is with "the primitive," "the natural," "the childlike," or that situated outside the cultural circle
- Drug experiences, trances, or transcendental experiences
- Peak experiences—sublime, perfect, or harmonious experiences
- The hybrid, the totally meaningless, that which lies beyond the categories of language

In all these cases, the intention is to break down conventional categories of meaning. Through a disturbance of the senses—what surrealists called *dépayser*—possibilities open up for giving new meaning to experience, from which new concepts arise. What breaks through, according to this mythology, is a more honest, more authentic "self" uncorrupted by civilization, convention, or neurosis.

The Original and Natural

The object in these cultural negotiations is to create signs and symbols of these liminal experiences, which in turn create in us a state of "authenticity." We can recognize such strategies in both jazz and music therapy, whether in the many myths surrounding musicians and the forms of music or in the choice of instruments and musical material. Such strategies are well known in the total emotional, verbal, and mythical discourse about these musical cultural forms.

Berkaak defined the preliminal as the creation of "an original context for the interpretation of ongoing action and identity" (Berkaak, 1993, p. 195). In the jazz world, we find such strategies when critics, and sometimes musicians, describe jazz as a "primitive" form of art or music. For example, French jazz critic Hugues Panassie (1971) described Louie Armstrong in terms that bear witness to the cultivation of the jazz musician as "the noble savage," a person more in contact with "humanity" than is the deformed, civilized European:

> One feels the intensity with which he lives each moment; one feels his innate goodness, his uprightness, his simplicity. Gifted with an extremely lively sensibility, his reactions are immediate and attractive in their finesse, spontaneity and intuition. He approaches people and things with his entire humanity . . . music is such a natural part of him that he no longer feels the need to talk about it, just as one does not talk about the air one breathes (pp. 23–24, quoted in Gioia, 1998, p. 19).

In music therapy, similar preliminal strategies can be observed when the therapist emphasizes the regressive aspect of therapy, in which the client returns to childlike behaviors—spontaneity, irresponsibility, and so on. When we "act like a child," we create a context in which we can act more "naturally," more "in accord with our innermost feelings." This regression is also liminal because it allows us to experience the world from a completely new perspective. In the words of Lilli Friedemann (1974), one of the pioneers in German so-called collective improvisation:

> . . . improvisation has a liberating effect. It is an action in which one can be playful and wholly human at the same time. The improvisation can level out the effects of one-sided intellectual education.

To become fully human, we must disregard the intellectual perspective and become a child. The childlike perspective counteracts all fragmentation and intellectualization.

The instruments and musical material we use also help establish the preliminary atmosphere. We can choose ethnic instruments, or those inspired by such instruments and adapted for educational purposes. Orff instruments, which have been adopted by a great many music therapists, were inspired by African instruments. Music therapists have become dependent on world music wholesale catalogs. Therapeutic improvisations often use the melodic and rhythmic material found in ethnic musical forms.

Music therapists metaphorize the musical material itself, so that it emphasizes aspects of nature or the body. "Rhythm is life," Hegi wrote (1986, p. 32), going on to describe how rhythm is attached to body functions, the change of seasons, and conditions in nature. In this cosmology, the experience of rhythm is connected directly to health, and pathology is viewed as a disturbance in the "rhythms of life." He saw a connection between disturbances in the "rhythms of life" and the diseases of modern civilization, including obesity, heart failure, respiratory problems, sleeplessness, apathy, drug dependence, depression, and suicidal tendencies. We are like drum skins eventually broken by our own vibrations. Therapeutic instruction in improvisational exercises is seen as a tool for recalibrating the "rhythm of the body" (Hegi, 1986, p. 35).

The Spontaneous, Immediate, and Nonreflexive

Sub- or prestructural categories are apparent in jazz and music therapy in the spontaneous, immediate nature of improvisation. For instance, Panassie wrote:

> In music, primitive man generally has greater talent than civilized man. An excess of culture atrophies inspiration, and men crammed with culture tend too much to play tricks, to place inspiration by lush technique under which one finds music stripped of real vitality (Gioia, 1988, pp. 29–30).

In this rhetoric, the techniques and specialized knowledge of culture are regarded as hindrances to spontaneity and intuition, and civilization has replaced vitality with illusion. The ideal seems to be expression without cultural competence.

When saxophone player Sonny Criss had the honor of playing with Charlie Parker for the first time, he concentrated on mastering the technical challenges of bop. "I was trying really hard," Criss remembers, until Parker reprimanded him: "Don't think. Quit thinkin' " (Leonard, 1987, p. 74).

Because improvisation is an oral form of expression in which the music is not necessarily based on a written score, improvisation fits easily into this romantic mythology. *"Zugleich sind aber die meisten davon stilistiche Merkmale abßereuropäischer Musik, die nicht nach Noten gespielt wird"* ("This is even a stylistic characteristic of most of the music outside Europe, which is played without a written score"), Friedemann wrote. In other words, consciousness of the oral aspect of this music has been significant for this pioneer in improvisational music therapy (Friedemann, 1974, p. 8).

I remember that when we established our training program in music therapy at a music conservatory in Oslo (Østlandets Musikkonservatorium), the other teachers joked that we ran a sort of musical kindergarten. In other words, in a serious institution for music education that cultivated classical bourgeois education built on such values as duty and exercise, music therapy was distinguished by its anti-elite values. It became a virtue in our program to develop a form of musical interaction in which everybody could participate, even without any previous formal training or knowledge. It became central to our ideology that everyone could take part in our musical activities regardless of psychological, physical, or social presuppositions. In music therapy, total democracy with respect to musical interaction became a norm. Classically oriented musicians, however, regarded this democratization as a threatening vulgarity.

The Transcendent, Peak Experiences, and Trances

Berkaak defined the transcendent type of liminality as superstructural—that is, as a way of aiming at the absolute as an ideal in itself (Berkaak, 1989, p. 206). In music therapy, certain peak experiences are classified as religious experiences. Leaving improvisational music therapy for a moment, let us look at an example of transcendent experience in receptive music therapy, taken from Helen Bonny's Guided Imagery and Music. One of the participants in a session described the following experience after having heard Beethoven's *Emperor Concerto*:

> Eventually, I heard the opening strains of the slow move-
> ment of Beethoven's *Emperor Concerto*, welcomed them,
> and experienced an aesthetically pleasing sense of *flowing*
> [italics mine] with the music. Caught up in its relentless,
> yet gentle, motion, I was carried higher and higher towards
> some ethereal, pure white mountaintop, bathed in golden
> sunlight (Bonny and Savary, 1973, p. 125).

The space is here sensed as being above reality, as something pure white, filled with the aesthetically pleasing experience of "flow."

Improvisational music therapists often work together with clients who cannot speak. Therefore, we have to interpret facial expressions or musical engagement in order to document peak experiences. An explicit aim of music therapy is to give patients such transcendental experiences.

Music therapists also refer to what Berkaak called the extrastructural, dramatizing the world that lies outside ordinary rationality and order: the wild, untamed, and intense. Berkaak suggested that all trains of thought are invalid because they represent reasons for action and experience that lie outside the individual and therefore may be felt as "inhibiting" (Berkaak, 1989, p. 211). The ideal state is trance and transcendence, in which the experience of "communitas" is realized (Berkaak, 1989, p. 214).

Norwegian composer and jazz theorist Bjørn Kruse also emphasized that the concept of "stream of consciousness" is attached to creative improvisation but is often interpreted as "stream of unconsciousness" in the sense that it is close to a meditative process—a kind of artistic glossolalia (Kruse, 1990–1991, p. 9). Jazz violinist Stephane Grapelli put it like this:

> Improvisation—it's like a mystery.... When I improvise and
> I'm in good form, I'm like somebody half sleeping. I even
> forget there are people in front of me. Great improvisers are

like priests: they are thinking only of their god (Leonard, 1987, p. 74).

Roy Eldridge described how he "saw the light" when he played with Gene Krupa:

> I'd fall to pieces. The first three or four bars of my first solo I'd shake like a leaf, and you could hear it. Then this light would surround me, and it would seem as if there wasn't any band there, and I'd go right through and be all right. It was something I never understood (Leonard, 1987, p. 72).

Great jazz musicians often go into trances. Louie Armstrong once told trombonist Trummy Young:

> When I go on the bandstand, I don't know nobody's out there. I don't even know you're playing with me. Play good and it will help me. I don't know you're there. I'm just playing.

Jazz historian Robert Goffin (1944) associated Armstrong's talent with just this quality:

> Louis possesses the great gift which permits him almost automatically to enter into a trance and then to express his sensibility by means of his instrument. . . . I know of no white musician who is able to forget himself, to create his own atmosphere, and to whip himself up into a state of complete *frenzy* (p. 167, quoted in Gioia, 1988, p. 30 [italics mine]).

When we remind ourselves that the word *frenzy* has connotations of "temporary insanity, paroxysm of mania, delirious fury or agitation, wild folly" (*The Concise Oxford Dictionary*), we understand the powerful forces released through improvisation. Here, we meet musicality beyond the border of madness; it is a journey into insanity, with an almost out-of-control aggression.

Paul Nordoff once told me that he could forget about the outer world and find himself in the same "inspired state" experienced by his clients. Remarks like this showed his spiritual kinship with such mystical traditions as Sufism. For a period, Clive Robbins used to end our meetings by reading from the *Tales of the Sufi.*

In the transcendent state, improvisation can be likened to a drug experience. In fact, Hegi, a Swiss jazz musician and music therapist, compared the force of the drug experience of addicts with the musical intoxication of intense improvisations. Astonishingly, this intensity seems to replace the need for drugs, Hegi wrote (1986, p. 19). It was experiences like this that led Hegi to redefine his work. He took free improvisation out of its purely musical context and into a therapeutic one—and became one of the leading music therapists in Switzerland.

According to Berkaak, we can also add such themes as energy, animals, nature, or even death to the category of extra-structural liminal references. Many of these themes are of central importance in music therapy: often, clients adopt the role of an animal during an improvisation. In Chapter 10, see the case example featuring the client's bear and bird images. British music therapist Mary Priestley wrote the following as a commentary on my narrative of the case:

> . . . I must admit I am intrigued by the improvisations on the bear and the bird because a patient of mine, who did very well indeed, also did improvisations on these two creatures. We reversed the roles between us. He became altogether more bear and less bird. He chose them himself; perhaps they have archetypal significance in this hemisphere and are included in the folklore of the north (personal correspondence, March 7, 1978).

Although the theme of nature often provides an associative point of departure for improvisation, death can also become an important theme for therapy (Kenny, 1982).

"Communitas"

Instead of "aesthetic refinement," improvisations in music therapy seek to build a community ("communitas") through a temporary leveling-out of all social roles. During improvisation, all traditional expectations regarding the role of therapist do not apply: music therapists try to build a spontaneous, immediate community through "free collective improvisations," in which complementary symmetrical forms of social interaction originate spontaneously out of musical interaction. Improvisation becomes a joint project in which emotion is the main measure of the credibility of the experience. In this way, music therapy has something in common with romantic mythology: it is skeptical of language and the intellect's control over reality. Improvisation is described as being more honest than language because music can express what is feared or hidden by language and intellect.

This liminal experience of closeness and mutuality between people is what Turner called "communitas": "These individuals are not segmented into roles and status but confront each other rather in the manner of Martin Buber's I and Thou" (Turner, 1969, p. 132). Typical of this experience is the direct, immediate, and total confrontation of identities. Buber also emphasizes that an immediacy; a sheer sense of presence; and a lack of aims, means, and anticipation are necessary before a "meeting" can take place (Buber, 1968). Turner's spontaneous or existential "communitas" is an especially appropriate description of improvisation—the spirit of community before the introduction of rules and social systems. Buber's view fits well with the humanistic ideology of music therapy, which posits the subject–subject relationship as the norm for therapeutic relations, exactly as it is experienced in improvisation.

When we try to relate the specific musical aspects of the improvisation to the liminal aspects of the I–Thou, we can again focus on the aspect of "flow"—the timeless—that seems to constitute the core of spontaneous "communitas." In Turner's words (1969):

> . . . in passing from structure to structure, many rituals pass through communitas. Communitas is almost always thought of or portrayed by actors as a timeless condition, an eternal now, as "a moment in and out of time," or as a state to which the structural view of time is not applicable (p. 238).

In this "eternal now," the other subject appears as Thou. Buber also defines this appearance as an aspect outside of time, as an incidence beyond cause and effect. When we try to fix a Thou in time, it becomes an It. When reading Buber, we again find the conception of the "meanwhile," the time between, experienced as "flow," an indefinable "void" or empty space, a point with no coordinates (Buber, 1968, p. 31).

This moment is known to jazz critics and music therapists alike. Commenting on Thad Jones's description (above) of being in touch with "fellow musicians," Norwegian musicologist Kjell Oversand (1987) used terms that evoke Turner's "communitas" experiences:

> What counts here is the aesthetics of the presence. You have to give yourself totally, without reservations. Attitudes like egoism, possessive feelings, and the spirit of competition have to give way to generosity, closeness, and communion. You develop a presence close to telepathic intuition. It is not enough that you believe this or that is going to happen. By beholding behind the closed eyes of your co-musicians, and in sensing the nerve impulses and the movements of the muscles in their bodies, you will attain a security in relation to what is going to happen. In such moments improvisation is like the language that spontaneously originates between two lovers, and what is usually called eroticism (pp. 74–75 [my translation]).

In this description, the experience of "communitas" is taken into the realm of the erotic, sensibility has gone under the skin, and the feeling of communion has attained a telepathic dimension.

Buber's work has often been invoked as a witness of truth, in refutation of behavior therapy and its ambition of programming and conditioning all aspects of life. By supposing that the Thou can exist only in a mutual, unconditional relationship, all attempts to inscribe the therapeutic relationship in an object-world are invalidated. In letting the unpredictable improvisation establish the frame for interaction, we have created a counterposition to the positivist ideal of predicting and controlling human relationships. (This is one of the main points of my book *Music Therapy and Its Relationship to Current Treatment Theories* [Ruud, 1980b, p. 40].) If the essential aspect of therapy is seen as changing the relationship to "one's self," then the liminal aspects of improvisation keep this channel of communication open.

TRANSFORMATION

Improvisation makes change possible, *with or without therapeutic consequences.* In jazz, this is often described as a peak experience in which participants live a drama that leads to the acknowledgment of wholeness, meaning, self-awareness, and so on. A good illustration is the ultimate meeting rock musician David Crosby (of Crosby, Stills, Nash, and Young) had with John Coltrane, "live" at a toilet in a jazz club in Chicago. In his biography, Crosby informs us that he was full of drugs before he was taken to this club "on the South Side . . . to a club called McKey's which was at 163rd and Cottage Grove, which I can say is very far down. Very far. We were absolutely, I swear to you on my word of honor, the only three white people in there" (Crosby and Gottlieb, 1988, p. 64). Both the outer and inner conditions necessary for a ritual journey were present. After Coltrane and McCoy Tyner had both performed, Crosby was literally driven out the room by the intensity of Elvin Jones's drums. He had to flee to the restroom to handle the situation:

> I was leaning my head against the cool vomit-green tile and drawing deep breaths, trying to calm down, when the door went *wham!* and in walks John Coltrane, still playing at top intensity and volume, totally into it. He blew me out so bad I slid down the wall. The guy was still playing his solo. He hadn't stopped. I don't think he ever knew I was in that room. He never saw that little ofay kid in the corner, you know, but he totally turned my mind to Jell-O at that point and that was my John Coltrane experience (pp. 65–66).

The experience was beyond any attempt at categorization, beyond even the liminal—so intense that Crosby experienced a mental meltdown.

I have a chapter to add to the "Coltrane Tales." In the early 1960s, Coltrane visited Oslo with the same quartet described by Crosby. We were a group of teenagers, who for a period gathered around the record player each Saturday night to listen to Coltrane. We had established our own little "communitas," a jazz avant-garde outpost on the east side of Oslo. After the concert, one of the consecrated was actually allowed to help Elvin Jones with his drums. Afterward, our fellow worshiper adopted the habit of talking about "Elvin and I," which was perceived by the rest of us as an improper infiltration into an a sacred community by an unworthy mortal. The episode generated an unusual number of witty comments for quite some time.

Coltrane was probably aware of the manifold of followers he had gathered, even though he did not have any well-defined intentions about his music communicated. When Coltrane was asked if he consciously tried to lift or influence his audience, or if he felt any responsibility toward his followers, he expressed a true Rogerian "nondirective" attitude:

> Sure, I feel this, and this is one of the things I am concerned about now. I just don't know how to go about this. . . . I think it's going to have to be very subtle; you can't ram philosophies down anybody's throat, and the music is enough! That's philosophy. I think the best thing I can do at this time is to try to get myself in shape and know myself. If I can do that, then I'll just play, you see, and leave it at that. I believe that will do it, if I really can get myself and be just as I feel I should be and play it. And I think they'll get, because music goes a long way—it can influence (Kofsky, 1970, p. 241).

Coltrane did not wish to force a ready-made theory on anyone, and he did not support the prevailing categorical ways of thinking. Henri Bergson's concept of intuitive understanding is close to Coltrane's epistemology. He was perplexed about just how he should influence others, so he chose the Socratic "know thyself"— transformation would originate in the listener when Coltrane's music flowed freely because he was in touch with himself.

The character and scope of transformation comes into question when we evaluate the liminal. We need to discuss what is meant by transformation both in delineating the sublime in relation to the liminal and in therapy, where we must determine whether "ritual" change is endurable and profound or only temporary. Anthropologists have also questioned whether the ritual process really involves a transformation, or if it deals with only the transportation from one state to another and back again

(Myerhoff, 1990). The "as if" character of the rituals might mean that even though they can be dramatic, jazz experiences leave only more or less lasting impressions—or can we really say that such moments act as incentives for us to alter crucial aspects of our basic outlook on life?

This question addresses a main theme in arts therapy theory, although it seems to play a minor role in anthropology theory. In addressing the transformational effects of the liminal, we are once again confronted with the question of reflexivity because, as anthropologist Barbara Myerhoff suggested, there emerges a definite contrast between "flow" and "reflexivity." This means that the ritual presupposes that thought and control must be played down to allow the liminal to appear. At the same time, reflexive attention (especially on the part of the therapist) is perceived as necessary for instigating permanent change. Allowing oneself to be caught up in the ritual process while still maintaining some distance—that is, to use what Mircea Eliade described as "archaic techniques of controlled ecstasy"—is vitally important for the therapist. (For a discussion of the relationship between music therapy and shamanism, see Moreno, 1988.) This is especially the case in those forms of improvisational group therapy in which the therapist carries the responsibility of both leading and fueling the creative group processes as well as of maintaining control and an overview of the situation. It is probably through this practice that music therapy can encounter problems with the surrounding reality—that is, with so-called scientific credibility and acceptance by "mainstream" health-care providers.

From Chaos to Structure

A therapist with therapeutic self-experience and knowledge of a client's history and behavior, however, is not led by the method but strikes a balance between structure and antistructure in improvisation. As Turner (1969) wrote:

> Wisdom is always to find the appropriate relationship between structure and communitas under the given circumstances of time and place, to accept each modality when it is paramount without rejecting the other, and not to cling to one when its present impetus is spent (p. 139).

An example from the work of Norwegian music therapist Ruth Eckhoff illustrates this point. On the basis of the psychoanalytic theory of object-relations, she uses improvisation into her work with psychotic clients (Eckhoff, 1991). These are people, to stay with the terminology, who live in a permanent liminality, where there are no boundaries between me and not-me and where surroundings seem threatening from the chaotic, unstructured perspective of these clients. Of course, the task with these clients is not to create another "void" through uninhibited "flow," but rather to help the clients organize their psychic life in a more formal and conventional direction, by using structured improvisation.

Myerhoff, in her article, asked what is meant by *transformation*. What is it that undergoes a transformation—self-awareness, state of consciousness, beliefs, feelings, knowledge, or understanding? If we were to let the music therapist answer, she would suggest a pattern of transformation experienced at different levels. Eckhoff builds her theoretical model on five levels of *experience in depth*. The nonpsychotic neurotic client seeking behavioral or emotional change may (1) be formal, be polite, or play a role; (2) be emotionally involved (here and now); (3) act symbolically or through processes of transference; (4) be controlled by archaic feelings; or (5) lose control and act out. When working with psychotics, however, Eckhoff moves strategically from step 5 to step 1.

This model tells us something about possible different levels in the liminal experience. It also tells us that by changing strategies—from the structured to the free, from the programmatic to the associative—we can create in-depth experiences in which the processes of transformation coincide with the needs of the client.

From Chaos to "Communitas"

In Eckhoff's work, improvisation is followed by verbal interaction, which orientation toward reality is explicitly tied to language and everyday life. In other words, reflexivity is taken care of through language. Our question here is if the musical improvisation, as a *nonverbal* process, can initiate change or transformational processes.

The following excerpt from a case study of improvisational music therapy with a client without language shows that our model of interpretation can explain even basic change. Here, Nordoff and Robbins (1971) describe a session with 9-year-old boy with Down syndrome as an example of the response category of "chaotic-creative beating":

> It is important that this child be musically stimulated—he himself must be allowed to improvise. The therapist does not try to impose musical order, for this would inhibit the *inherent* creativeness of the child's ego. The responsive work of the therapist precipitates moments of musical perception which lead the child to relate his beating to the improvisation. At first these *fleeting responses* consist of only one or two musically related beats, but they form the basis for therapeutic work which gradually secures the child's confidence in himself. He feels himself within the music and in beating can exteriorize his experience. He enjoys the musical give-and-take and anticipates the next working session . . . . His musical intelligence is realized gradually and the *intimate rapport* consolidates the work. Response 3, Limited Rhythmic Freedom, becomes established. A *musical companionship* arises which makes further therapeutic coactivity possible (p. 72 [italics mine]).

This music therapy allegory contains several of the elements we have described in the framework of a rite of passage. The child is free to express himself through a supposed inborn creative ability tied to his ego—"a dynamic source of complex rhythmic impulses lived within him" (Nordoff and Robbins, 1971, p. 28). Thus, the musical material is linked to the preliminal, to a kind of "real human nature" that is present in spite of "extremely limited possibilities and very little speech." In other words, the child's expression is not only more original but is also an expression freed from cultural competence. In another commentary on the case, we read:

> In response to the improvisation he would play impulsive rhythmic patterns and intricate syncopation. His "music" was *free, playful, and completely unpredictable*, yet it bore a *fragmented rhythmic structure* that was related to the

improvisation. . . . He seemed to be at that stage of *inner chaos* where creative freedom merges into *incomprehensibility* and *incoherence*. The drum-beating was not at first consciously self-directed activity for this boy. He was *utterly absorbed* in realizing expression of the rhythmic impulses that lived within him. Consciousness of what he was doing developed later in the session as he experienced his beating impulses being answered in the music that surrounded him. When this happened, and the boy and I *really met* in the music, the activity that had been a *playful and unpredictable* game began to take on the form of a musical give and take (Nordoff and Robbins, 1971, pp. 28–29 [italics mine]).

The introductory phase is marked by the unpredictable and fragmented chaos at the edge of the comprehensible. At the very threshold (*limen*) of the meaningless and disconnected, where we hear not music but "music," the boy experiences a form of reflexivity in which he recognizes himself through the music that comes to him. This experience of recognition, in which the undefined and chaotic spontaneous inner life finds an answer in an outer form (that is, in Nordoff's improvisation), leads to order and mutuality—"a musical give and take."

This mutuality also has the characteristics of "communitas": "When this happened and the boy and I *really* met in the music," Nordoff recalls [italics mine]. He reveals that the improvisation also resembles Buber's "meeting." The experience is "real" in a way that is distinct from everyday reality. The music therapist–pianist has stepped out of a formal role and his musical interaction with the boy has become a relationship on equal terms, one of "intimate rapport" and "musical companionship." After the improvisation (reaggregation), a general change in the boy's behavior is noted: "Towards the end of the work, one of the teachers noticed a change in the boy. In his daily life he seemed generally more awake and purposeful" (Nordoff and Robbins, 1971, p. 29).

The transformation here takes place through a nonverbal process. Reflexivity is created by recognition, when the child notices that his own categories of experience are reflected in his experience of the music, or vice versa. In the debate between therapists about the role of verbalization in music therapy (music *as* therapy versus music *in* therapy), this case is an example of how change can occur without categorizing the experience by verbal concepts. The concept of "intuitive perception," developed by French philosopher Bergson, is relevant here. It points to the fact that all verbal acknowledgment presupposes the acknowledgment of a spontaneous character, an intuitive acknowledgment that grabs hold of the phenomena—especially music—in its movement, transience, and transformation.

Myerhoff commented that the processes of transformation that emerge in performance rituals can never can be forced (Myerhoff, 1990, p. 246). Thus, transformation is seldom an explicit goal for such rituals, although it is expected that the ritual changes the person's position or status. Turner's concept of "communitas" was influenced by Buber's "philosophy of the meeting," which deals specifically with this unconstrained aspect of I–Thou. Buber wrote that such "meetings" happen only through *grace* (see also Bollnow, 1969), which reminds us that we cannot plan or plot such experiences.

Chapter 9

IMPROVISATION
AS SOCIAL INTERACTION, OR
GETTING INTO THE "GROOVE"
OF MUSIC THERAPY

This chapter and the next are based on my experiences as a music therapist for young or adolescent boys with behavior and emotional problems. In discussing two sessions, I will try to address some of the questions raised in earlier chapters, such as the nature of music in music therapy, how we go about translating the session into a descriptive and theory-laden written form, and how musical processes in themselves may lead to those changes in behavior we label "therapeutic." Both chapters are more theoretical than clinical, in that descriptions of the clinical situations serve as a point of departure for theoretical discussions. In other words, they should not be read as traditional case studies.

In this chapter, I will describe in some detail an improvisational music therapy session with a 14-year-old boy. My intention is not to describe a successful intervention but to focus on the way we use language when we retell the story of an improvisation in words. In this sense, the process of writing down this story became an exercise in reflexivity in which I tried to show that concepts from interaction and communication theory were useful in evaluating this client. This showed me that an improvisation can be described in the same terms used to describe early-infancy interaction. Furthermore, it helped me to focus on the musical processes involved—how we both were caught up in a common musical "groove." The nature of this experience, which made a lasting impression on me, highlighted the question of how music can become "therapy" through the mutual confirmation of two people participating in and sharing musical expression.

CASE STUDY

Jim was referred to me from a psychiatric day center where I worked part time with adolescent boys with behavioral problems. He was a large, clumsy, extremely insecure boy, difficult to engage in meaningful conversation. He had a history of severe learning difficulties, refusing to take interest in anything other than geography. He had taken piano lessons some years before I started to work with him, but he was neither interested in talking about them nor willing to demonstrate what he had learned.

During our first session, he sat on a sofa on the other side of the room, inactive and refusing to cooperate. He was threatened by the situation. I did not interfere with him, only playing music to him. He did not like my repertoire and stated that he was not interested in what I had to offer him. In the third session, the piano's mechanics broke down and I had to open the piano and loosen one of the keys. Jim became very curious. He approached me; after I had shown him the inside of the piano, he was more willing to talk to me. He said his only musical interest was in disco music and that he wanted to learn "disco style" at the piano. I found this request rather challenging and asked him to demonstrate what he meant. He had developed a distinct rhythmic piano style based on repetitive chords composed mainly of fourths and fifths, which clearly referred to the rhythmic aspect of disco music, leaving out both bass and melody. When I asked him to sing in "disco style," his performance showed that his concept of the music was very much colored by his habit of sitting between the amplifiers at home, probably with a high bass volume. He seemed to have no sense of melody.

From this rapport based on disco, we went on to agree that *he* should teach me disco style and that we could then play together. In the terms discussed in earlier chapters in this book, Jim had found his musical identity in disco music. Severed from society by his personal anxiety, this identity was a refuge where his identity as a youth could be maintained, his personal space secure from invasion by impending adulthood.

Jim's condition was diagnosed as borderline, and he had psychotic outbreaks, especially during clay modeling classes. As part of his social training program, he began coming to my studio at the conservatory each week for about 45 minutes. He never showed any sign of losing control during the year he visited me. He was extremely excited on certain occasions, however, standing up from the piano stool and waving his arms. He was quite easy to calm. His movements outside the music room were generally restricted. With his head down, he would drag himself slowly along the wall of a long corridor in the conservatory, never showing any outward signs of excitement or energy. The energetic and definitely rhythmic potential that he demonstrated in improvisation contrasted sharply with this behavior.

After several weeks, he started to play from his small repertoire of improvised music, allowing me to use the tape recorder. One of his favorites was a modified and improvised version of the first page of the first movement of Beethoven's *Moonlight Sonata*. He resisted any of my attempts to engage him in formal learning. He would not learn the names of the keys, bring any printed music to session, or play melodies. He would only play chords and improvise with me rhythmically.

I decided to focus on the following therapeutic goals: to improve his communication competence and to expand his ability to follow instructions, lead, and take initiative. I saw as an important short-term goal that he learn to trust an adult and gradually accept responsibility for learning new communicative and musical skills.

Sessions were generally not too eventful. Sometimes we stopped after half an hour. Other times, we decided to go beyond the prescribed 45 minutes. Much of the time was spent listening to the recording of the session and talking about the music. One particular improvisation, however, was particularly powerful. I will describe this in more detail, although as will be evident, the core of the music can never be successfully represented in any language or notational system.

This particular improvisation had a three-part structure: A, B, C. The first part, A, was characterized by distinct rhythmic descant disco chords interacting with a rhythmic descending stepwise melody in the lower register of the piano (my part). What strikes me when I listen to this dialogue is its disruptive character. The two parts never came together harmoniously; both parts fought for dominance or flew away from each other. Clearly, each time there seemed to be a musical agreement, a temporary rest in a certain key, Jim broke away, often raising the key a half tone. Thus, it became increasingly difficult for me to transpose the descending melodic line. At certain points, I did succeed in creating a harmonic counterpoint to Jim's prevailing rhythmic stereotypes, creating a sort of cadence. Often, the improvisation broke down completely. The breakdown can be interpreted not only in communicative terms but also on the basis of a lack of technical and musical skills and resources to fulfill a piano improvisation, or it may also be a demonstration of the lack of code competency on my part—I failed to fall into the disco groove.

Although the disco mode did create a secure space for Jim, a referential code, there were too many uncertainties to make the music a safe place (see Kenny, 1989, p. 79). The possibilities for stylistic changes were too many; the redundancy was not sufficient to create an elegant, musically smooth interaction. The personal tension was intermingled with the stylistic complexity; the flow of musical information was too unpredictable to allow either of us to foresee the next step of the other. Jim seemed to have a sense of rhythmic timing, however, thus creating interesting harmonic-rhythmic tension, yet although improvisation is usually conceived of as a dialogue, this one was marked by its mostly asymmetric character. The two parts could not be classified as complementary. There was too much tension and mutual chasing to allow our play to be categorized as our seeking to complement each other.

In the B section, however, complementary play seemed to occur; the character of the improvisation changed. I found the situation unbearable, the tension too hard to maintain. Slowly, the improvisation led up to a "cha-cha-cha," introducing a popular Norwegian song. This tune invited Jim to successfully imitate and respond more directly to the code. From my point of view, it was also an effort to break out of the restricted code, the disco mode, which was the basis for our musical contract but also tyrannized all our improvisations. Responding to the cha-cha-cha, Jim again found a safe space and proved he could cooperate, follow instructions, and let himself be led. The situation became quite humorous, me deliberately playing wrong notes, singing, and inviting Jim to respond freely. In the language of communication theory, this was clearly a complementary situation, a follow-the-leader game in which Jim had to be the leader.

In the final section, C, I set out to further jazzify a popular Norwegian children's tune and I challenged Jim to give not only a rhythmic response but also a melodic one. This challenge represented a threat to his safe disco-youth identity, but the improvisation succeeded, probably because of the jazz-disco stylizing of the childish song. Although initiative leads to complementary communication, Jim was able to fill in with rhythmic riffs in a way that made the improvisation truly symmetrical. He even tried to use his fingers successively instead of playing his stereotyped chords all the time. At the remarkable climax of the improvisation, we both stopped, anticipating and predicting each other's stylistic interpretation, thus demonstrating the creation of a common musical code, or the mutual taking of the other's perspective.

DISCUSSION

When I look back on this improvisation, listening again to the tapes and reading my own description and interpretation, I asked myself the following questions: How are the three parts of the improvisation different? If my perception of the first part is of a somewhat flawed improvisation, on what evidence do I base my perception? What was missing in part A, and how and why did the improvisation improve later in the session?

In my description, I stressed the lack of complementary interaction, the disruptive, struggling character. There were difficulties when we tried to establish a common beat, which led to a breakdown of musical narrative or completion. There was rhythm without pulse, high intensity with no resolution. In the second part, however, there a dialogue began. In the emergence of musical fill-ins, there was a growing sense of turn-taking. The imitation had a somewhat teasing character, and there was no element of struggle. This led to a more fulfilling musical narrative, although it was musically conventional. The beat was steady and the interaction had a complementary character. Intensity seemed low, however, and Jim took a very compliant role, letting me take control of the course of the music. In part C, I continued to lead the improvisation, but I raised the level of intensity. The basic beat was driving, and both narrative and completion were present and fully developed. The pattern of communication became more symmetrical. Although I took a leading role, Jim's creative initiatives demonstrated that he understood my musical intentions. He fulfilled the musical expectations and even manipulated and played with them. Most important, our levels of intensity seemed to match; there was a sense of attunement stemming from the common flow of beat, intensity, and narrative.

When we deconstruct the language used in this presentation, we can detect many levels of descriptive and interpretative language. In my first description, I tried to stick to musical language, talking about rhythm, key, transposition, beat, musical imitation, and so on. In my commentary, I consciously used the terminology of interaction and communication theory: turn-taking, dialogue, imitation, affect attunement, pulse, intensity, narrative, complementary and symmetrical communication.

I have the following reasons for trying this experiment in reflexivity. I want to see if categories taken from recent interaction theory make sense when applied to a description of a music therapy improvisation. Because developmental psychologists have for a long time borrowed concepts and metaphors from music theory to make sense of what goes on between mother and child in the first months of life, it seems fair to see if this playing with metaphors aids our understanding when turned the other way around. We use metaphors to make sense of, structure, order, or create meaning in a field. A metaphor (literally, a carrier) transports meaning from one area to another, thus making us look at the world in a particular way. One objection to the use of the metaphors of developmental psychology might be that music is not infant interaction, just as infant interaction is not music. On the other hand, we run into difficulty if we think that either phenomenon could be described literally. Even the language of music theory is a metaphoric language: an F♯ is not a sharp F.

A point of departure for this discussion might be to try to find support for the argument that music itself has some therapeutic value, as I discussed in Chapter 5. If human communication in general is made of the same stuff as musical communication, music therapists do not merely conduct improvisations with clients—they communicate. In this sense, musical communication is an exercise in human interaction.

MUSICAL DIALOGUE: AN EXERCISE
IN COMMUNICATION

This session of musical dialoguing in a music therapy session clearly illustrates the possibility of developing a relationship between two people through music, a feeling of participation and togetherness despite an initial distrust, a lack of common goals, or a common understanding of the situation. This phenomenon illustrates one of the basic problems in sociology and psychology: how do we learn the game of social interaction? How do people in general develop mutual understanding and predictable, trusting relationships on which to build a personal or social organization?

Music has long been recognized in the social sciences as a kind of protocommunication. In the article "Making Music Together—A Study in Social Relationships," distinguished phenomenological sociologist Alfred Schütz (1951) treated music as a form of social interaction that precedes verbal communication:

> As far as the question under scrutiny is concerned, the concrete research of many sociologists and philosophers has aimed at certain forms of social intercourse which necessarily precede all communication. Wiese's "contact situations," Scheler's perceptual theory of the alter ego, to a certain extent Cooley's concept of face-to-face relationships, Malinowski's interpretation of speech as originating within the situation determined by social interaction, Sartre's basic concept of "looking at the other and being looked at by the other" (*le regard*)—all these are just few examples of the endeavor to investigate what might be called "mutual tuning-in relationships" by which the "I" and the "Thou" are experienced by both participants as a "We" in vivid presence (pp. 78–79 [my paraphrasing]).

Such precommunicative social relationships can be conceived of in terms of musical dialogue, as "mutual tuning-in relationships, which originate in the possibility of living together simultaneously in spe-

cific dimensions of time" (Schütz, 1951, p. 78). *Time,* of course, is a
key concept. Phenomenologically speaking, the question of "Why
music in music therapy?" can be reduced to music's temporal
structure.

Looking back at the case study, we see that it is exactly this
live experience of mutual tuning-in through time that happens
toward the end of the improvisation. In listening to the tape, I
find evidence of a reciprocal intentionality in the changes in harmony, melodic and rhythmic fill-ins, and the increasing incidence
of musical understanding.

Schütz's analysis, however, focuses on the communication
between composer and listener. He argued (Schütz, 1951) that the
"we" basic to all communication can be thought of as a "mutual
tuning-in" to the experience of time:

> We therefore have the following situation: two series of
> events in inner time—one belonging to the composer's
> stream of consciousness, the other to the beholder's—are
> lived through in a simultaneity created by the ongoing flux
> of the musical process. It is the thesis of the present paper
> that this sharing of the other's flux of experience in inner
> time, this living through a vivid present in common, con-
> stitutes what we called in our introductory paragraphs
> mutual tuning-in relationships, the experience of the "We"
> that is at the foundation of all possible communication.
> The peculiarity of the musical process of communication
> consists in the essentially polythetic character of the com-
> municated content—that is, in the fact that both the flux
> of the musical events and the activities by which they are
> communicated belong to the dimension of inner time (pp.
> 78–79 [my paraphrasing])

This "we" is empirically evident in my exchange with Jim because
of the inherent participatory nature of improvisation. Owing to its
emphasis on the composer-listener situation, Schütz's analysis
can take us no further in our understanding of improvisational
communication, but Schütz's phenomenological social research
laid the ground for such important work as Peter Berger and
Thomas Luckman's theory of the social construction of reality.
This may be what we have in mind when we consider not only

how communication is socially constructed in interaction between people but also how nonverbal communication in musical situations is represented in a verbal mode, influenced by the social character of language.

We can find similar thoughts about communication in the work of other sociologists. Niklas Luhmann, a communication sociologist, emphasized that social systems have evolved from mutual uncertainty and unpredictable situations (see Østerberg, 1988, Chapter 11). Those who have taken part in "free collective or group improvisation" in music therapy may have experienced the process that leads from total chaos to consensus within a common code or structure. Such group improvisations can be seen as examples of the art of social organization. (For further reading, see Lecourt, 1994). In the case study presented in this chapter, the same feeling of chaos was present in the opening section of the improvisation.

Improvisational music therapy is thus like a miniature social system. This reference to sociological theory is important if we accept some of my premises about music therapy as concerning social groups or society at large. What I refer to as the "laboratory of music therapy"—the close clinical setting—may be regarded as a place to model or construct some of the tools the client needs to become involved in a larger social system. As a musical laboratory, music therapy can be used, as demonstrated in my case study, to investigate how musical dialoguing through Creative Music Therapy techniques is developed and maintained.

Generally, however, there seems to be no strong tradition in either sociology or psychology for studying musical communication or improvisation to better understand communication in general. There has recently been a strong interest, though, from developmental psychology and interaction theorists in using metaphors from music to describe early interaction between mother and child. (Thanks to my colleague Jon-Roar Bjørkvold for bringing to my attention the themes common to musicology and interaction theory [see Bjørkvold, 1989, 1992].) Researchers Colwyn Trevarthen and Daniel Stern both contributed to this trend. Many music therapists have pointed out that their way of describing mother–child interaction is very similar to the musical behavior observed in a clinical improvisation. In the following discussion, I will present some aspects of this theory that relate to

the case study outlined earlier in this chapter. It is important, however, that we not forget the actual musical reality experienced.

THE DIALOGICAL MIND

One way to understand how a child grasps the rules of the
game is to apply G. H. Mead's theory of "taking the perspective of the
other." Mead explained that the child, by taking the perspective of
the other, can predict the other person's reactions to her own actions.
As a result, she can modify her actions. This ability to take someone
else's perspective seems to be a basic prerequisite for communication
in general; people who are communicating need to foresee reactions
and regulate their behavior toward each other.

Mead's theory, however, was based on a mediated communication in which language or other systems of symbols created a
presupposition for communication. This dependence on semantic
systems also led Schütz (1951) to look to music for a kind of protocommunication:

> In any case, the existence of a semantic system—be it the
> "conversation of significant gestures," "the rules of the game,"
> or "language proper"—is simply presupposed as something
> given from the outset, and the problem of "significance"
> remains unquestioned. The reason for this is quite clear. In
> the social world into which we are born, language (in the
> broadest sense) is admittedly the paramount vehicle of com-
> munication; its conceptual structure and its power of typifi-
> cation make it an outstanding tool for conveying meaning.
> There is even a strong tendency in contemporary thought to
> identify meaning with its semantic expression and to consider
> language, speech, symbols, and significant gestures as the
> fundamental condition of social intercourse as such (pp. 77–78
> [my paraphrasing).

The interest in looking to music for adequate metaphors to describe infant interaction points to the importance of the nonsemantic
or more immediate character of early communication. Norwegian
sociologist Stein Bråten also stressed the unmediated communication
sometimes seen as a dialogical dance, giving an impression of the

immediate and nonsymbolic (Bråten, 1990, p. 110). From this observation, he went on to ask the important question of what basic constitutive processes underlie this ability to take another's perspective. For him, the answer lay in postulating a primary dyadic organization of the mind as a presupposition for engaging in the mutual interaction that eventually leads to the life world of a common language. For music therapy, it seems natural to support such a hypothesis. As improvisation demonstrates, there is frequent nonverbal and immediate communication—the musical taking of the role of the other—in music therapy. Improvisation also makes sense pragmatically in light of Mead's theory; it helps the child exercise this basic role-playing.

Continuing in this vein, musical elements can be related to early communication in terms of temporal aspect, dynamic qualities, and narrative form. The first dimension concerns such musical parameters as tempo, beat, and rhythm. For instance, Trevarthen emphasized, in a seminar on Music and Infant Interaction he conducted in Oslo in May 1997, the basic sense of timing and beat in early interaction. If we plot the interaction between mother and infant on a regular time scale, we will see similarities to a musical score. Daniel Stern called this sense of timing an important step in the child's development of the capacity to read interpersonal processes as "protonarratives" (Stern, 1996). In other words, the mutuality of communication can be seen as if it has some kind of dramatic tension built into its structure; the peaks and release of tension are part of the narrative time structure. There is an element of improvisation between infant and adult in which the infant learns to predict coming events, lets itself be surprised by unexpected events, and, most important, develops intentionality. The child also develops some sort of "relational knowledge"—that is, how it feels to be with another person. This sense of intersubjectivity is further stimulated by the affective attunement of the mother, often drawing on the way she reads the intensity and dynamics of the infant's expression or the timbre of the vocal expression.

PUNCTUATION

Schütz's view of the immediacy of protocommunication not based on the mediation of verbal language is evident in Trevarthen's and Stern's descriptions of an infant's interaction with her mother as a spontaneous skill not dependent on learning or culture, at least in the first months of the life. This predilection for immediacy may lead music therapists to think of music as a kind of "natural language," thus perhaps romanticizing music into a noncultural object. In other words, the question to be raised in the following discussion is: To what extent do musical language and the "flow" of improvisation depend on the mutual sharing or learning of culturally constructed codes? If we grant that there is an element of immediacy, represented through musical "tacit knowledge" founded in the nonreflexive performance of the body, then the next question is: If this tacit communication competence, as represented in musical communication, is a part of the newborn's repertoire, how is this spontaneous unmediated knowledge transformed into a culturally constructed rule-based musical code?

To begin with, we must accept that there are always some reactions to music that are not cognitively processed. Although music psychologist Harold E. Fiske based his theory of musical cognition on the mind's ability to discern between properties of the musical object, he talked about a level of experience similar to the psychological phenomenon of "cocktail party" perception (Fiske, 1993). In other words, we may be aware of objects and phenomena in our surroundings without being able to name or place them. We may notice changes in our living room—an object moved—without being able to pinpoint exactly what has changed. In a similar way, we may respond to music in ways not "style conscious" or based on code recognition. We merely respond spontaneously to some flow of information, responding with our bodies intuitively, in an unmediated way, especially during improvisations in which we are unfamiliar with the musical or improvisational idiom or when changes in the music call for reorientation. It may be, however, that when there is musical interaction between an adult and an infant or between a music therapist and a severely handicapped or cognitively impaired person, this is *our* way of categorizing the interaction as "musical" rather than the actual lived experience of the child or other person. We may talk about "musiclike" ways of interacting, using music interactional flow as a metaphor for what is going on. We can never know, however, to what extent our categorizing has general validity for others' experiential worlds. I propose that improvisations in general are built on the mutual sharing of culturally constructed intentions.

Improvisation involves learning a musical code, the rules necessary to create a meaningful dialogue within a particular musical style. Learning the rules through musical turn-taking can be explained with such concepts from communication theory as punctuation, symmetrical and complementary communication, and representation. To master the rules of musical communication is to master the rules of punctuation set by the participants during the improvisation. As discussed in the previous section, a successful musical dialogue may depend on a presence of a common code of musical understanding that allows the mutual prediction of musical phrases. Thus, improvisation can be compared to play, with its possibilities and probabilities and continuous variation in the flow between certainty and uncertainty.

One way to rework this type of musical interaction into a theory of communication is simply to regard it as learning. In the discussion here, the musical improvisation is analyzed using concepts derived from Gregory Bateson's theory of learning and communication (Bateson, 1973b).

People participating in improvisational music therapy, whether children or adults, have widely different backgrounds in music (Ruud, 1986, 1989). The therapist usually has a strong background in music—technical and musical skills and the ability to express a wide variety of musical elements. Children's levels of musical skill or competence vary a great deal. At one extreme are children who are almost musically inexperienced, if that is possible in our society. They come to therapy without any—or certainly without rigid—ideas with respect to what music can or should be. Other children have mastered musical codes at a level close to or equal that of the music therapist, with the rest falling somewhere in between.

Let us consider the situation when the music therapist is confronted with a child with little or "no" musical skills. How do children learn? What does the child have to learn before we can really say that we can communicate with her? Learning and communication are closely tied to each other. Bateson supposed that learning itself is a phenomenon of communication. (See also Ølgaard, 1986, p. 96.) Reading the literature of learning theory led

Bateson to suppose that there is a hierarchy of forms of learning, ranging from "zero" learning to a fourth degree of learning. Zero learning became the notion for actions that are not subject to change through trial and error and that involve an automatic, specific, or genetically determined response. Zero learning in music therapy would simply imply a level at which music is used only as a means of getting the client's attention.

For a child without any experience with music, the sounds produced by the therapist might appear meaningless—without order, connection, or definite intentions. The child might ask: Why is that person touching that "table"? What shall I do with these "sticks"? Why should I beat these round boxes?

We can imagine that at this level, it is the sound itself that will first fascinate the child. It is the "difference" from other more "daily" sounds that attracts attention. The quality of sounds from particular instruments is also used by the music therapist to arouse attention. In the beginning of music therapy, the first step would be to grab the child's attention by using sounds that are different from any sound the child has previously heard. At this point, though, the therapist still would not have achieved more than fascinating the child, focusing her perception on an aspect of her surroundings.

We may argue that this achievement would have a "therapeutic quality" in certain contexts but a limited therapeutic value if we want the child to act intentionally in certain ways. In other words, what we wish to see is the child revealing that she has understood that a sound can be combined with another sound in a way we find meaningful. Because we are members of a certain musical culture, we have learned the rules of how sounds can be combined and have mastered the concepts or "frames" for how the connections between sounds can be perceived, interpreted, and understood. For music therapy, Bateson's first-degree learning would be parallel to classical conditioning, a way of modifying zero learning. Learning is not specific to the situation; it is a generalized reaction that encompasses a greater variety of responses and expectations. Evidence of first-degree learning in music therapy is when the child perceives music as a signal referring to "It's time for music." Music thus creates an important frame or "context marker" for the following interpretation.

What appears to *us* as evident, as the most obvious and predictable connection between tones, may not necessarily be perceived as reasonable to the child, however. Our problem, then, is not only to try to get the child to understand or perceive *our* kind of order, our ways of combining tones. We also must help the child understand that there is something to be understood as "order." Put another way, we are giving the child not only the presuppositions necessary to participate in a certain musical culture but also the necessary qualifications to understand that it is possible to create an order between sounds that can be perceived as meaningful.

It is hardly possible to imagine that the child can perceive such an order without the existence of certain inborn biological features common to human beings. Such similarities do not, however, imply more than the ability to hear differences and to understand that different stimuli can give rise to certain patterns. We are compelled to suppose that such a perception of "pattern" is possible for all people— that all people find interest and pleasure in holding on to such patterns, follow developments in pattern organization, combine patterns, predict the continuation of patterns, or arrange patterns into a larger whole. If this level of attention is reached—if the child can perceive differences—we can go on to speculate how the communication situation develops.

Let us focus on the point in an improvisation when our efforts are directed at helping the child understand and apply the musical code. To overcome this challenge, the child would have to apply, in Bateson's terms, "learning of a second degree." This may be understood as a change in the way we mark or segment the flow of impression, how we apply the context markers. In other words, second-degree learning can be seen as changes in the punctuation of learning contexts.

To better understand second-degree learning, let us take a closer look at musical interaction. Imagine a "flow of sounds" between child and therapist. What may happen is that the therapist hears certain melodic and rhythmic patterns, a certain melodic phrasing, dynamic expressions, and so on. The improvisation is already meaningful to the therapist because it can be understood and seen within a certain frame, or within a musical cultural context. At the same time the therapist may perceive the improvisation as frustrating because of a lack of consequence in the exchange of sounds. The therapist must constantly change perspective to meet and interpret stimuli so that they will be perceived as meaningful. The therapist will look for a perspective or a musical frame of reference to cling to, a certain way to bring order to the sounds or patterns.

In this free exchange, the child or the therapist will soon begin to stress when a certain pattern stops or begins—in other words, to signal that there shall be a pattern and how this pattern is constituted. This is a phase of "punctuation," placing "period" and "comma," or trying to form an agreement about which order to follow (see Watzlawick, 1976). Because this is a dialogue, the therapist must be careful to create rules of punctuation that are understandable to the child.

The music itself offers possibilities for an unlimited number of punctuation systems. Let us imagine that in this stream of sounds, there appear differences in pitch, loudness, tone qualities, and dynamics. A rhythm such as xxxo xxxo xxxo is likely to be perceived as a pattern, especially if it is performed like this: xxxO xxxO xxxO. If, in addition, we put a new tone quality at O, like xxxØ xxxØ xxxØ, or stress both sounds melodically and harmonically, like xxxY xxxY xxxY, the likelihood increases that the child will sooner or later perceive this figure as a certain pattern and will start to expect a similar progression in the musical dialogue. At this point, the therapist has created a frame within which this particular music is to be perceived, giving the child a certain perspective from which to arrange the music. The therapist has arranged or punctuated the sound impressions in such a way that a certain meaning or narrative is possible if this order is followed.

Violation of this order, as in xx\\ x\xxx, may lead to confusion, to a new orientation, but the therapist has already come far in establishing a communication situation. If the child follows this narrative—what the therapist, by the way, will control empirically when the child beats the drum at the "right place" in the improvisation—the child has learned some rules or codes not only for musical communication but also for communication in general. She has learned to take the perspective of the other and has experienced the meaning to be found in fulfilling, filling out, challenging, and perhaps changing this order.

In future improvisations, the child might overcome her frustrations because she has experienced numerous possibilities for organization and might begin to find pleasure and meaning in joining the therapist in making new rules of punctuation or developing new perspectives on the organization of the musical material. Indeed, a long period of improvisation may follow, representing a search through the possibilities for organization.

It is easy to see that these improvisations can come to illustrate communication in general, in which either the child or the adult may take the lead. Communication then becomes both symmetrical and complementary. This analysis points to the fact that in improvisation, there are signals that mark a change of perspective. There must also be signals that invite playing with musical frames or patterns. Again, we can seek help from Bateson, in his theory of play and fantasy, to study improvisation further. He held that in play, we can find messages at different levels, from simple signals (mood signs), to messages that simulate such simple signals, to messages that determine which of the two other types is operating (Bateson, 1973a). Beating a drum may be a way of expressing anger, or it may just connote anger. We need cues to tell us if the drum-beating is meant to as anger or its musical representation. When I said that the child must learn some kind of order to understand how to behave in a situation, this can be understood in terms of how the child must learn to distinguish between logical types. The concept of *logical types,* which Bateson borrowed from Bertrand Russel, informs us that a class cannot be a member of its own class. According to Bateson, communication must take place at several logical levels at the same time, and there must be signals that show what kind of logical type is represented by the signal in question.

If music is a kind of language, it is situated somewhere between gestures and verbal or discursive symbols. This transitional status makes it similar to play, which can also be seen as a form of transition leading to language. In this way, play itself can be seen as helpful for the child in her process of mastering the perception of different logical types. In the play, the child investigates the borders between objects and symbols (Hohr, 1990, p. 107).

GETTING INTO THE GROOVE

Returning to the session with Jim, we can now see how this improvisation makes sense when regarded as a method of communication, or rather as a way to communicate about communication in a nonverbal, sometimes intuitive or immediate manner. It also seems reasonable to deduce from the improvisation that it resulted in a strong moment of meaning and mutual affirmation. The core of the musical situation lies in the moments of the last section when there was an intense rhythmic flow, a real participation, full of what Charles Keil conceptualized as "participatory discrepancies." Keil argued that the heart of the meaning of music lies not in its notational structure but in its performance aspects (Keil, 1987; Keil and Feld, 1994). Those experiences that lead to involvement and participation in music originate from a mutual sense of playing around the beat and out of tune. This performative musical discourse around a set of culturally established musical codes emerges in milliseconds and microintervals. Playing "on the top" (a little ahead of the beat) versus "laid back," the particularly "chunky sound of the bass," the "missing notes" of Miles Davis (see Walser, 1995), the "grainy voice" (Barthes, 1977) of a vocal performer, and so on are evidence of and give significance to these events. It is likely that no analysis of excerpts from a musical improvisation would catch those microseconds of mutual understanding and coactivity that lead to "meaningful moments" (Amir, 1992). This is the dilemma of any attempt to analyze music therapy situations within the frames of the traditional musicological analytical apparatus. Efforts at such transcription and analysis (see Chapter 10), despite their sophistication, advanced terminology, and triangulated cross-references, may risk loss of those microseconds of rhythmical discrepancies or particular out-of-tune references that are the essence of the participatory musical experience. The musical participation in process has been taken up by another distinguished ethnomusicologist, Steven Feld, who has shown that this analytical approach may help us to tease out the symbolic meaning of musical practices in a cultural group (Feld, 1984; Keil and Feld, 1994).

I hypothesize that the concept of "participatory discrepancies" goes right to the heart of Paul Nordoff and Clive Robbins's work with exceptional children. Unlike Keil and Feld, Nordoff was not an intimate fan of the African-American musical tradition. He never, as far as I know, expressed affection for the work of Aretha Franklin, Thelonius Monk, or James Brown. He was an exceptional classical composer, and his love of popular music extended to the Tin Pan Alley genre. He brought his classical background to his free improvisations with children. He would set the beat in a romantic, slightly dissonant modernist tradition. The melodic quality of his songs clearly showed his gift for creating popular tunes.

The "participatory groove" goes beyond African-American heritage, however, although it is probably more clearly demonstrable in the oral music tradition, as well as in music as performed in general. Nordoff and Robbins's music therapy practice took an oral improvisational approach. Of course, the two therapists placed great emphasis on recording, analysis, and transcription. Recording and notational technologies were meant to be used as further input in the oral evolution of the musical improvisation; sometimes only the heart of the piece was recorded by notation for publication as a musical piece.

It is my impression, after listening to many of the original tapes from these founding years, that the enthusiasm stemming from the improvisations with the children have their roots in the "swing" or "groove" of the musical interaction. Those happy moments of anticipation and surprise, those moments of reaching and going beyond the expected, and those openings that were to be filled in by the children can be regarded as evidence of a musical performance tradition manifested as the power to get people to participate.

The skeptical music therapist may of course say, "Yes—so what? Is this therapy? Do people really change?" My answer would have to be that there seems to be support in clinical theory for the idea that it is exactly these moments of mutuality, confirmation, and meaning or of "being seen," touched, or understood that lead to change, self-understanding, or self-acceptance.

Israeli music therapist Dorit Amir focused on what she called "meaningful moments" in music therapy: significant events in the process as experienced both by therapists and clients (Amir, 1992). In her dissertation, she also referred to several authors from the fields of psychology and music therapy, from Maslow to Rogers, who stressed this part of the therapy process. There may be many terms for these moments, ranging from Abraham Maslow's "peak experiences," to Rollo May's "pregnant moments," to various religious and mystical descriptions.

Because this chapter has examined improvisation from the perspective of interaction theory, I propose that we can liken the musical peaks of an improvisation to the possible moments of meaning in the interaction between infant and adult. I find support for my argument in Daniel Stern's theory of "hot present moments," which I find comparable to moments of "participant discrepancies."

Stern began the discussion of his theory with how and why change occurs (Stern, 1996). From psychotherapy, we know change may occur when the unconscious becomes conscious, but many psychotherapists—and probably many music therapists—have felt that this is not the whole story. There must be something more. As psychotherapy research has shown, clients may recall, many years after actual therapy sessions, that some special moments in sessions, especially in their relationship with the therapist, contributed to the change process. These meaningful moments, or moments of presence, were linked to the client's perception of the relationship with the therapist as an authentic, "real" relationship. An important element in this relationship would have to be the therapist's courage to disclose himself, to be really present, much in the same sense as Buber's "meeting." In contrast to much existential theorizing about these moments in the literature, Stern's view was that they were everyday experiences, confirmations of intersubjectivity.

Adult–infant interaction can be compared to an improvisation process in which two people are moving toward a more or less definite goal. Sometimes the only purpose of the interaction is fooling around together—having fun and entertaining each other. Typical of this kind of unstructured, aimless interplay are spontaneity and accidents, episodes of trial and error in which interaction fails, has to be repaired, or is momentarily chaotic. This form of improvised interaction, understood by Stern as a complex dynamic system, creates new moments of intersubjectivity and a new context for interaction.

It is exactly those moments when intersubjectivity is confirmed that Stern is concerned with. In such situations, we may feel how something important is going to happen. Stern called this going through a "pregnancy phase." This is followed by the "weird phase," a feeling of being unable to define the situation, which confuses us and makes us seek a way out. In the crucial "decision phase," we choose a solution to the situation: to enter a confirming meeting with the other or to withdraw or create some other "flawed moment." If we choose the latter, we are back to the starting point, as if nothing really important had happened. If this moment—Stern's "now moment"—is transformed into a "hot present moment," we have created a new intersubjective frame for the interaction, and the goal for the interaction may change.

Stern sought to understand these "hot moments," wondering if any knowledge from musicology could clarify them. I suggest that musical improvisation itself provides many metaphors that allow us to understand these moments. Improvisation may be characterized by an aimless, sometimes chaotic way of playing together, but it often develop to a point when recognition, expectation, and choice can create both pregnant and "weird" moments that will either be spoiled or produce strong, confirming moments of meaning. In other words, a musical "hot moment" in improvisation, which is similar to the experience of "swing" or "groove" in popular music, may help us understand how people can change after they have been in improvisational music therapy. This is surely an important aspect of "music as therapy."

Chapter 10

IMPROVISATION
AS PLAY AND FANTASY

For the humanistic music therapist, music is not only a tonal constellation but also an expressive medium, a kind of language situated somewhere between gestures and verbal symbols. This transitional status makes music similar to play, which sometimes can be seen as a form of transition leading to imagined ways of being. Sometimes this play, or musical improvisation, can help children master the borders between fantasy and reality.

This chapter, based on a session from another case study, reflects on the possible transition from music to semantics. Before presenting the case, I will discuss the use of musical analysis in music therapy. Again, my focus is the nature of music and musical communication and the way we as music therapists represent and translate our improvisations into the language of therapy.

PHENOMENOLOGY AND ANALYSIS
IN MUSIC THERAPY

From a musicological point of view, improvisation in music therapy may not be "interesting" in the same way as a major piece of art music. Improvisation does not generally produce a musical work of art. Thus, some analytical procedures from traditional musical analysis may not be relevant. Even if such methods might indicate structural idiosyncrasies of the improvisation, we do not use them to see how certain features may organize the musical text or what stylistic features are operating and how they are historically related. Instead, we study how music provokes inter- or intrapersonal communication—in other words, which musical structures will lead to change or a new initiative. It is also important to state something about the relationship between the expression we read in the music and the communication the client possibly intended. Furthermore, our reading of the improvisation serves as a basis for discussing likely therapeutic consequences or initiatives.

Thus, improvisation interests us on three levels:

- *The structural level.* Any improvisation has a certain form and an idiosyncratic musical organization, as does a musical work of art. This means it is possible to describe and analyze the music in purely musical terms. In such an analysis, the emphasis should be on the musical processes that lead to personal interaction between client and therapist. We must be aware of some of the limitations of the analysis of notated music, however. As I discussed in the previous chapter, the performative qualities of music, which are not so easily captured by our conventional notational system, are what give meaning to music.
- *The semantic level.* We can do an analysis at two levels to find what different structures in music "mean" or what their significance is. We can look for "meaning" at the level of the relationship between the players or we can look for musical meaning in the traditional way—what the music expresses or symbolizes.
  - By relating the different musical initiatives to the interpersonal processes between client and therapist, we may be able to conclude something about what the different musical structures mean in relation to the interpersonal interaction.
  - Through interpreting musical structures and, if possible, relating these structures to verbal information from the client, we may be able to say something about what the music states, expresses, signals, or signifies.
- *The pragmatic level.* This level seems to be more poorly defined in musical analysis. In a music therapy context, it means to illustrate the effects of the improvisation, or how the improvisation relates to the treatment carrier of the client, which therapeutic functions and processes are involved, and so on.

Because improvisations are usually not written down, it seems reasonable to select a method of analysis based on the sound experience of music, although we do not have to exclude other methods, such as more traditional methods of analysis, which may add to phenomenological description and interpretation.

In my dissertation on music as communication, I suggested a five-step model in describing the musical aspects of improvisation in music therapy (Ruud, 1987, 1990a). If we use the phenomenological description of music suggested by Lawrence Ferrara (1984), improvisations can be studied from the structural, semantic, and pragmatic levels.

We may begin by listening to an improvisation "openly," in the sense of trying to avoid any preestablished expectations or prejudices. The next step would be to attempt to identify the structural aspects—its musical codes—such as tempo, modality, texture, and rhythm.

It should be noted that phenomenologists are sometimes too optimistic about being able to "neutrally" describe music. A criticism of phenomenology in general is its effort to place certain types of information in brackets. It seems more sensible to speak about changing our perspective when we listen to music, focusing on different aspects of or levels in the music. We cannot become objective by magically dissolving certain types of experience. Instead, we must admit that it is not possible to listen to music without some sort of perspective. In other words, we cannot perceive "music as such," yet we can change our perspective to compare information obtained from different ways of listening. In this way, we can reach an understanding that, if not objective, is perhaps more comprehensive than would otherwise be the case. We can approach "objectivity" by investigating our perspectives, discussing the theoretical presuppositions of the analyst. This promotes documentation or controlled subjectivity, as discussed in Chapter 7. We must never forget, however, that we translate musical experiences into our own theory-laden language.

Although we may never perceive "pure sound," or whatever we want to call it, we can perceive sounds characterized in certain ways: cold sounds, warm sounds, dark sounds, bright sounds, large sounds, small sounds, metallic sounds, and so on. In other words, we must include semantic aspects in the description of sound. This is illustrated in Ferrara's own analysis (1984) of

Edgar Varèse's *Poème Électronique*. Approaching the description of the structural level, he wrote:

> Listening for syntactical meaning alone was a difficult task because of the often obvious semantic meanings to which the sounds referred. It was not possible to bracket out semantic meanings to which the sounds referred, although at several points during this listening it was startling to hear the sounds purely as such (p. 364).

The structural or syntactic description should be clearly set off from the next steps, which include speculations about meaning and expression. It seems to me that this description of a territory of an observed musical code, where we can claim or reach inter-subjectivity, is a necessary if our description is to achieve scientific credibility. Included in this concept of science is a necessary element of intersubjectivity, or at least the possibility of checking that our way of seeing the reality is the same that observed by fellow music therapists. In this way, we might describe elements of the music that could lead to significant changes in the client's behavior, which might in turn lead to changes in behavior defined as "therapeutic."

The next step in the research or listening process would be to investigate what the music expresses—the "meaning" of the improvisation. On this semantic level, we must infer from both the nature of the music and our knowledge of the patient what the music expresses. Of course, this part of the interpretation is highly charged with the possibility of overinterpretation. If the description is to claim any scientific value, it is vital that the process of description leading to a statement of "meaning" is discussed with regard to the client's musical cultural background, her present psychological makeup, and the therapeutic or interpretative concepts used by the music therapist (his affiliation with a specific therapeutic system).

After a discussion of the improvisation's semantic aspect, there must be a statement of how this particular musical expression is related to the client's therapeutic carrier. This pragmatic aspect must be stated nondogmatically to make explicit that the theoretical constructs used in the observation or description of music and behavior are methodological concepts created to understand the behavior, the experience, and changes in the client's behavior. The last step in the analytical procedure implies a final "open listening" to sum up and to see whether our interpretations have changed.

DESCRIBING THE IMPROVISATION: SOME METHODOLOGICAL ASPECTS

The first step in the analysis of an improvisation, even before the first open listening, is to write down the associations and information particular to the situation immediately after the session. This information will be very important, of course, for further interpretations at both semantic and pragmatic levels. It may also add to the controlled subjectivity and thus the credibility of the interpretation. To the extent that we want to say something about what music expresses, both our own associations and intentions as well as any statements from the client help reduce arbitrary interpretations. Any comments from participants might be regarded as a composer's spontaneous comments on her creative process. Especially because music therapy deals with how personal expressions are triggered by and contained in musical structures, this information is important if we want to read the music's symbolic content. A general description and evaluation should be followed by observations of the client in different situations, which should lead to concrete suggestions about the goals of the work.

Any effort at observation is of course problematic because observation depends on a theoretical language or model. This also holds true for any statement about the character of music. Because of this, there will always be a need to reflect on the nature of our theories. For music therapists, then, discussion of the status of the philosophy of science related to our concepts and observational procedures is just as important as courses in therapy and self-experience.

When we listen to musical events and interaction, an important question is this: What part of the session will we describe and present? The answer depends on the purpose of the analysis, which must also be made explicit. We often select sections of sessions that are too long. Remember that sessions generally last from 20 to 40 minutes, during which moods change, different instruments can be heard, and initiatives come and go, so replaying the whole session may confuse the listener. This makes it difficult to define and get an overview of the situation.

Before editing the tape, we should write a short description of the whole session. Often, events can be ordered in sections, which may be only a few minutes or seconds long. If there is only monotonous activity throughout the session (in which case we might ask other questions), it is not necessary to present more than a few seconds to illustrate what is going on. Furthermore, we must always provide information about who was playing when and what and about who was situated where in the room.

Those "interesting" incidences during the session that are relevant to our goals are the moments we want to preserve, investigate closer, and communicate. So that we can study them, those seconds or minutes should be edited on a separate tape and commented on further. Important questions are: What is happening musically and how might I describe in musical terms what is going on? What does this mean in the relationship between client and therapist? What is happening in the client's mind in reaction to the musical event? Because we never truly know anything about what the client experiences unless she tells us, we may have to study the musical events as they occur and relate them to any signals we received from the client. At this point, some music therapists conclude too much, especially when they do not have the client's own verbal expression to support their statement. They draw conclusions without critically examining the interpretation or their own theoretical presuppositions.

Our *research* task is to explain why music has a therapeutic effect. In other words, when something interesting happens and we can describe its difference from the usual interaction, we describe its nature or, more important, what caused the difference to arise—what happened in the musical interaction or in the relationship between client and therapist that led to the change. This is the core of the description. Because this chain of communication cannot be seen in terms of a cause and effect relationship, we must relate to it as an infinite resource. Because it may be impossible to detect the "first" cause, we may try to base our analysis on a certain incidence in the chain of communication and describe those signals or *markers of context* we may interpret as the events leading to changes.

Doing research on the musical material implies the use of verbal translations, however. This does not mean that we must engage in any kind of mysticism or explanations pointing to some hidden or universal meaning in music. Instead, we can closely examine the musical codes in operation. We can ask how these codes are established, whether they originate in the client's sociomusical background as parts of the general musical codes of her culture, whether they are learned in the therapy session, whether they are private, and so forth. Just as we might engage in a discourse about symptoms, observations, interpretations, ideologies of therapy, and concepts of health and illness, we can engage in a discourse about the possible qualities of music, aesthetics of music, or theories about the sociological and psychological foundations of music.

The discussion above should be seen in light of Chapter 9. As I concluded here, it is possible to argue that improvisations provide a context for a nonverbal, mutual confirmation—that there is a kind of "music as therapy" going on. In this sense, the experience of mutuality is "verified" not through verbal statements but through the felt experience of mutual recognition through musical interaction.

THE BEAR AND THE BIRD

The following is a detailed analysis of a session from music therapy. The emphasis is on the musical facet of the improvisation; I will not discuss in detail the therapeutic results. My aim is to provide a phenomenological description of what is happening at the musical level and to relate this to possible changes at the intra- or interpersonal level. Then, I will suggest likely interpretations of what fantasies the client's musical expressions may represent. Keep in mind that my focus is further thoughts on the nature of music in therapy.

In this description, I will try not to use terms already burdened by theoretical or clinical theory (for instance, psychoanalysis). Most of the time, I will try to use concepts defined within the context, to meet the need for documentation or empiricism. That is, instead of saying that some passages are influenced by primary process thought, I prefer to say something like "During this section, we can imagine that the client is associating so and so." If we want to categorize some associations or musical processes as "primary processes," it is a question of which theoretical perspectives we are willing to choose.

Although the emphasis is on the musical processes, we must consider the clinical or therapeutic context of this work. That is, we must be aware of the client's life history as well as the clinical goals or pragmatic issues of the improvisation. Jack was referred to me for music therapy when he was 7, already having a long history of contact with mental health services. Although he had severe behavioral problems, he had shown an early talent for music.

As we know, children with behavioral problems often have problems following the rules of social interaction. Usually, it is easy to find incidences of maladaptive behavior in their case histories. As a music therapist, I rather prefer to stress the positive behavior the boy showed in music therapy sessions. He was a friendly, helpful, and charming little boy. Throughout the years he participated in music therapy, he never missed an appointment or was late. Early on, we made a contract and set up some rules. Of course, he tested these rules in the first few weeks, but his behavior was promptly met with a firm response. Soon, he started to act positively during sessions, thus illustrating that behavioral problems, to some extent, depend on context. Our weekly sessions became a safe, secure space in his life. I was someone he came to trust; the music became a space in which he could express himself, learn some new competencies, and develop trust in himself.

Generally, we classify our life histories into three areas: a biological, a personal, and a social history. For the music therapist, it might be relevant to also talk about a musical or musical cultural history. For Jack, incidences in all these areas added up to the background creating his problems:

- His biological history showed a small sight problem; he was later found to have minimal brain damage.
- His personal (or interpersonal) history showed early hospital trauma, communication problems, a period of selective mutism, self-destructive behavior, and nonselective forms of contact-seeking behavior.
- His social history indicated that he had no knowledge of his biological parents; the first year of his life was spent in

a hospital. He was placed in a foster home and was later adopted.

The session described below occurred after Jack had been in music therapy for 4 years. That particular morning, he did not want to go to school. His mother told me that the day before, he had been harassed by the other kids. He did want to have his music therapy session, however. Over the years, we had established a fixed procedure, almost a ritual, of starting in the instrument storage room, where he was allowed to select the instruments for the session. He could choose only two instruments; he usually spent a long time trying out and experimenting with all the instruments in the room. That morning, he had already made his choices. He resolutely picked up the Orff alto metallophone and a large Orff drum and two hard mallets. I played the piano, and the instruments were arranged so we would have as much eye contact as possible.

Sample 1

Jack starts the session by playing the metallophone with a figure based on the notes G, F, and A, a main motif for this section. At the piano, I comment on his play by using the high register of the piano. The music floats rhythmically with no distinct beat. Tonally, there is a kind of modal eolian flavor. This introduction takes about 11 seconds. It has a bright character, like an opening gesture. The musical phrase is reminiscent of someone bowing, stretching his hand out in welcome. This gesture also establishes the form of the improvisation as complementary. In communication terms, Jack is leading and my role is complementary—containing or supportive.

About the same time as the piano closes this introduction with a reversion of his motif into G-A-D, Jack announces: "Now the bear is coming."

Sample 2

After this bright, friendly opening, this statement undoubtedly signals that there is a story to be told. The initial musical rhetorical statement was only a polite introduction. Jack's determined choice of instruments, with the deliberate contrast between the drum and the melodic metallophone, emphasizes that he wants to express and formulate something.

The next 10-second period is dominated by the drum. With 14 resolute beats on the drum and a forceful crescendo, Jack illustrates the appearance of the bear. The beats are not set in a fixed pulse; they are rather declamatory. The metallophone is given an accidental function. On the piano, I immediately switch to the bass register. I have felt the dramatic tension and want to support and eventually hit the tonal core of the drum sound, the low G.

In communication terms, Jack is still leading and my role is complementary. Toward the end of the section, the two parts are more synchronized; the improvisation is more symmetrical.

On the semantic level, there is the dramatic, almost threatening character of the drum crescendo. The distinct conclusive statement—the controlled final aggressive last beat—leads to questions: What is going to happen? What does Jack imagine?

Sample 3

The next 26 seconds consist of three parts. In the first part, A, Jack performs a pregnant rhythmical and melodic motif. In the middle section, B, there is movement between the tones E and F and a scale movement from C to G. The last part, C, is introduced with a pointed beat on the drum, followed by a leaping melodic figure. The sequence is concluded with a glissando at the piano at the same time as Jack makes his next announcement. It sounds like "Someone is calling at the door," but it is impossible to hear exactly what he is saying.

Throughout the whole sequence, the initiatives come from Jack. The piano is supportive. Musically, note the use of chords composed of fourths. My intention here was to increase the tension. With this chord, it is not necessary to define the music's tonality, even though the metallophone part is in C major.

To begin with, it may be reasonable to interpret the rhythmic/melodic motif in part A as a gestalt of the idea either of the bear or someone approaching the door in order to see who is coming. Remember that this theme comes as an answer to the violent crescendo. The theme has a "brave" quality. The rhythm reminds me of a traditional Norwegian school song, based on the same rhythm, called "Courage in the Breast." If Jack is not the bear, it might be that he imagines himself approaching the bear. The bear, of course, is a very powerful symbol of strength. We might ask whether he is mixing the two roles; they are not that far apart. It is impossible to determine exactly what is going on in his fantasies. This points to some essential qualities of the nature of music: that the ambivalence inherent in musical "statements" makes possible changes or shifts at the level of fantasy and that music enables us to play different roles in relation to the same musical expression.

Part B in this sequence may reflect the particular ambivalence appearing in his fantasies. The indeterminate movement between E and F, supported by the tremolo on the piano, might illustrate how he needs time to differentiate the roles. Letting the scale go on beyond the octave might be a way of gaining time to define himself.

The tension created by the upward movement finds its resolution in another firm beat on the drum: this beat has now become a symbol for the bear, we might assume. This is again quickly accompanied by the low G on the piano; this time, I did not have to waste time finding the best supportive tone. The low G is followed by a melodic leap. I play chords of fourths under his melody.

Part C, which lasts for 31 seconds, introduces another musical signal, the sound of a doorbell. We also hear Jack actually announcing that someone is calling at the door. He then imitates the bell signature by repeating the C-G motif five times. The first two bell sounds are supported by dissonant chords in the piano. After the call signals, Jack calls out, "Now the bear is coming," which is again illustrated by the drum, this time with five beats. The piano imitates the drumbeats. Then Jack says with a theatrical, artificial adult voice, "Yes? Who is it?"

Sample 4

Owing to the sometimes bad recording, I must suggest other possible interpretations. When Jack said that someone was going to knock at the door, it is possible that he said my name, "Even."

Because this was "my" room, this would make sense. When he used the "grown-up" voice, he might have been trying to imitate my voice—or merely playing the role of the bear. We might also interpret the situation as if that he took enough security from my presence to allow the door to open for the bear. This interpretation might be seen as supported by the fact that he then introduced another animal in the story: a bird.

After the question "Yes? Who is it?" he answers, in his most childish voice, "It is a little bird." Now we understand that the bear was not outside the door but in the room. He has taken the strength of the bear in order to open the door for the little bird who timidly calls.

After the bird answers, we hear an illustrative phrase on the metallophone, a downward stepwise melodic movement followed by a broken G^9 chord (Sample 4). In this part, the piano is "mumbling" around the left hand's G-G#-A. Immediately after the broken chord, Jack shouts, "No!" supported by a strong beat on the drum. The piano fills up the short break by imitating the drumbeat. Then Jack shouts, "I do not want you here!" The section dissolves in dissonance.

The following section contains a long, predominantly stepwise melody played on the metallophone. The piano takes over the melody, supported by parallel fourths. After a few seconds, Jack suddenly starts to accompany the piano by playing on the wooden side of the metallophone. Then he exclaims, "Now he's coming!"

Sample 5

The melody played by on metallophone might be interpreted as the bird's reaction to "I do not want you here!"—an elegant flight away from threat. We might also infer that the short interludes give Jack time to associate around the story, to prepare his next move.

Sample 6

After these last five beats on the drum, we might wonder who is coming. So does Jack: "Who is it?" he asks. Again, he answers himself: "It is the little bird from the Congo." To underscore the drama, I play dissonant chords built by fourths at the same time Jack repeats "I do not want you here!" Again, he accentuates his statement by answering "No!" at the same time he beats the drum.

METAPHOR
AND REPRESENTATION

To illustrate some of the challenges we face when we try to describe, document, or interpret improvisations, I chose these few moments from the beginning of an improvisation that lasted a total of more than 20 minutes. How do we proceed from the structure of the music to possible fantasies, images, or associations by the client and the therapist? What I have included here illustrates how every step of description includes a possible interpretation. We can never be sure that the description of the client's music by another therapist is the same as what the client would give. In using an example from my own work, however, I am at least able to state with some "objectivity" the thoughts and associations of the therapist's part of the improvisation.

The very use of language to describe a musical process implies interpretation. As I remarked earlier about the nature of metaphor, words and concepts impose a certain meaning on the music. When I read my description, I can detect that I am constructing the subject, Jack, as a person who "signals," makes "determined choices," "expresses and formulates" himself, makes "declamatory and dramatic" statements, and so on. The whole system of metaphors gives the description a dramatic, almost theatrical character. On this semantic level, Jack even plays as if is making a physical gesture, stretching his hand out, making music with a "threatening" character and a "pointed" beat, whereas the piano is "supportive."

Through this system of metaphors, music is constructed as a way of communicating something about a person's inner life. It is important to remember that Jack does not give any information about the background of this constructed conflict between the bird and the bear. We have reason to believe that he does not even know what forces or figures these animals represent. We might speculate that he uses the animals as symbols or protagonists for forces he feels around or inside himself. It is also reasonable to believe that he identifies with both the bear and the bird. Through the bear and the drum, he is the strong character who is courageous enough to open up when someone calls; he faces the unknown. At the same time, he is the little bird wanting to be let in. By taking the role of the bear, he can be the big, ugly, bad boy who scares the hell out of the little help-less bird, but as a little bird, he can also maintain distance, flying away, as he illustrates with the melody played on the metallophone.

From the information I had, it was not possible to do any further interpretation. We know, however, that he had recently been harassed at school, so he might have needed to invent symbols to illustrate a fight between the strong and the weak, between the persecutor and the persecuted. We could read the symbols as representing deeper emotional conflicts about the themes of acceptance and rejection, trust, and emotional security. Because we know that these are themes from his personal and social history, this interpretation seems reasonable. This is a good illustration, then, of how music therapy deals with psychoanalytical work.

There is one caution, however: even if we read a client's body language, we do not know the client's intention. Psychotherapist Irvin D. Yalom (1997) convincingly showed how, even in verbal therapy, we may totally misinterpret the intentions behind a smile or a word. When it comes to music, the chances of misinterpretation are, of course, even greater. Going back to my original argument, we must understand not only how patterns are established as a code or frame from which to organize sounds but, of equal importance, how the sounds used in communication may be given a content taken from the situation—the playful interaction between client and therapist.

As we saw in the previous chapter, the organization of sounds that we call music may be rooted in the early dialogue between child and mother/father. Sounds can be said to structure the communication patterns, or time structure, between the people taking part in the dialogue. How we speak about music later in life, or how these sounds are represented in our consciousness, seems to depend on the social context in which we live and experience music and the language with which we describe these sounds.

This critical discussion does not weaken the possibility of therapeutic action through music. So far, I have said nothing about the pragmatic level of the analysis, the part that should reveal changes conducive to therapy. In general, I suggest that it is the ambivalent, polyvalent, or transitional nature of music that gives music it strength as a therapeutic medium. German psycho-therapist Jutta Baur-Morlok remarked how the art therapies are in a more favorable situation than is verbal psychotherapy. She said that because music therapy is a nonverbal therapy, it offers the advantage of a complementary medium to verbal language in which one's internal world can be expressed and communicated to others. On one hand, she wrote, an essential element of music therapy is to provide a pure, cathartic encounter that is experienced emotionally, on the level of primary process. On the other hand, there is an exchange between two levels of experience, one of music and one of language. What has been perceived on one level can be translated and transposed to the other level. This works in both directions: from the medium of music to verbal language and from verbal language to music (Baur-Morlok, 1996, p. 233). In other words, we can express ourselves through music and then later reflect on this spontaneous expression using words. I am not saying that art therapies always imply the use of words, but I believe they sometimes demand some sort of reflexivity on the client's behalf after the therapeutic intervention.

If we return to the question of how to characterize the nature of music as it is revealed in this analysis, it is evident that the arbitrariness of musical symbols makes possible the coding of multiple meaning. Jack is able to freely fantasize to the music. The character of music or musical symbols allows him to redefine the content or role of the symbols while he constructs his story. The analysis also shows, however, that Jack can draw on the cultural repertoire surrounding or encoded in the music. The drumbeat becomes the forceful symbol of strength anchored by the cultural stereotype of the bear. His leaping melodic line illustrates the elusive character of the bird. This points to the role of music in therapeutic improvisation as being similar to that of music in film. Music introduces and sets the mood of the film. It may illustrate the narrative, serve as a leitmotif, imitate movements, or characterize the psychological processes going on inside the characters.

Communication

One of the problems we encounter in applying the concept of communication in music therapy is the implication that music is a kind of language conveying or referring to a concrete message. Musical communication is thus sometimes understood within a linear, mechanistic model: a message is sent via music from an addresser to an addressee and passes through different kinds of filters (notation, instrument, acoustics, and so forth). When this transportation model is transferred to music therapy, it is even implied that music's effect on the listener is therapeutic. Such a model does not function especially well in improvisational music therapy because the client actively produces the musical material, thus affecting the communication process just as the therapist does. This calls for a circular model of communication.

Within a circular model, we find that both people act on each other through a certain code—music—and the message refers to a certain context. This context may be fantasies or cultural conventions, or a mix of both. Drawing on a model of communication suggested by linguist Roman Jacobsen, we might find the following elements in the process (compare Fiske, 1982):

	Referential	
Emotive	Poetic	Connotative
	Phatic	
	Metalingual	

The emotive function describes the relationship between the message and the addresser; the term *expressive* is often used to refer to this function. The function of the message is to communicate emotions, attitudes, status, class. These elements make the message uniquely the sender's. Emotive functions are always present in musical communication, at least as a part the musical identity revealed through the musical style or code. *Connotative* refers to the effect of the message on the addressee. This aspect is, of course, important to the music therapist's work. The referential function, the "reality orientation" of the message, is of top priority in objective, factual communication. This function may be seen in musical improvisation using musical codes referring to preestablished extramusical conventions, as when Jack used the symbol of a doorbell.

The phatic function keeps the channels of communication open and maintains the relationship between the people involved or merely confirms that communication is taking place. In musical dialogues, the redundancy or the predictability of the musical code indicates its phatic function. It may be wise, therefore, to sometimes stick to a naive, simplistic code just to keep the channels of musical communication open instead trying to impress the client with sophisticated jazz-elaborated improvisation. I suspect that a lot of what was going on between Jack and me had this function of keeping the improvisation going. I suppose that sometimes this level of communication gives the client time to fantasize and make choices about where to go in the narrative.

The metalingual function identifies the code being used. In other words, music therapists may employ any sound as a means of communication as long as the context or frame is identified.

Finally, the poetic function is the relationship of the message to itself. In aesthetic communication, this function is clearly central. It is involved when music creates a context in which play and fantasy allow for a symbolic exploration of reality. The poetic function thus points to some basic feature of music as a medium in communication therapy. It also helps us create a point of departure for understanding the role of fantasy and language in improvisation. When we describe music as a "presentative," nondiscursive symbol, we point to some of its characteristics as an aesthetic medium. By rewriting this aesthetic quality in terms of play and interaction, we can see more clearly how improvisation is a context within which to symbolically investigate and redefine realities.

Anthropologists have remarked that activities within the context of "play" are similar to what is going on outside the play activity—at the same time that play is exempt from the trivial consequences of real-life activities (Berkaak, 1989, p. 77). Through play, we create a dialogue with outside reality: we comment on this reality, change it symbolically, play roles, and so on, without running into the consequences of the real situation. Anthropologist Don Handelman further illustrated this cultural analytical understanding when he wrote that meta-messages can make the reality of play a medium of self-reflexivity. Messages of play "take apart the clockworks of reality and question their organization and indeed their very validity as human and cultural constructs," he wrote (Handelman, 1982, p. 163, quoted in Berkaak, 1989, p. 79).

Musical improvisation allows us to experiment with meaning, to invest our fantasies and test other possible ways of being. It may be seen in the same way as the playground of play therapy, but with music as the frame surrounding the investigation of biographical experiences. Improvisation made it possible for Jack to begin a process of reflection in which he could present to himself and others some of the external and internal forces that made his life so troublesome, perhaps sorting them out with help.

REFERENCES

Abu-Lughod L, Lutz CA (eds) 1990. *Language and the politics of emotion.* Cambridge, United Kingdom: Cambridge University Press.

Adorno TW (1978). Musik og sprog—et fragment. In Nielsen P (ed): *Musik og materialisme.* Copenhagen, Denmark: Borgen.

Aigen K (1994). The role of values in qualitative music therapy research. Paper presented at the First International Symposium for Qualitative Research in Music Therapy, Düsseldorf, Germany, July 29–30.

Aldridge D (1996). *Music therapy research and practice in medicine: from out of the silence.* London, United Kingdom: Jessica Kingsley.

Aldridge D (1994). Single case research designs for the creative arts therapist. *The Arts in Psychotherapy* 21(5):333–342.

Alvesson M, Sköldberg K (1994). *Tolkning och reflektion: Vetenskapsfilosofi och kvalitativ metod.* Lund, Sweden: Studentlitteratur.

Amir D (1994). Experiencing music therapy: meaningful moments in the music therapy process. Paper presented at the First International Symposium for Qualitative Research in Music Therapy, Düsseldorf, Germany: July 29–30.

Amir D (1992). Awakening and expanding the self: meaningful moments in the music therapy process as experienced and described by music therapists and music therapy clients. Ann Arbor, MI: UMI Dissertation Service.

Ansdell G (1995). Music for life: aspects of creative music therapy with adult clients. London, United Kingdom: Jessica Kingsley.

Antonovsky A (1991). *Hälsans mysterium* [*Unraveling the mystery of health*]. Köping, Sweden: Natur och kultur.

Assagioli R (1988). *Lo sviluppo transpersonale.* Rome, Italy: Astrolabio.

Barthes R (1977). *Image-music-text.* London, United Kingdom: Fontana Paperbacks.

Bateson G (1973a). A theory of play and fantasy. In: *Steps to an ecology of mind.* Frogmore, United Kingdom: Paladin.

Bateson G (1973b). The logical categories of learning and communication. In: *Steps to an ecology of mind.* Frogmore, United Kingdom: Paladin.

Baur-Morlok J (1996). Translations. In Langenberg M, Aigen K, Frommer J (eds): *Qualitative music therapy research: beginning dialogues.* Gilsum, NH: Barcelona Publishers.

Becker H (1982). *Art worlds.* Berkeley, CA: University of California Press.

Berkaak OA (1993). *Erfaringer fra risikosonen: opplevelse og stilutvikling i rock.* Oslo, Norway: Universitetsforlaget.

Berkaak OA (1992). Narrative and deconstructive strategies in visualizing cultural processes. In Crawford PI, Simonsen JK (eds): *Ethnographic film aesthetics and narrative traditions* (proceedings from NAFA 2). Århus, Denmark: Intervention Press.

Berkaak OA (1989). Erfaringer fra risikosonen: opplevelse, utforming og traderingsmønster i rock and roll. Unpublished doctoral dissertation, Department of Social Anthropology, University of Oslo, Norway.

Berkaak OA, Ruud E (1990). Kunstideologier og sosiale relasjoner i et rock and roll band. In Deichman-Sørensen T, Frønes I (eds): *Kulturanalyse*. Oslo, Norway: Gyldendal.

Berkaak OA, Ruud E (1994). *Sunwheels: historien om et rockeband*. Oslo, Norway: Universitetsforlaget.

Berkaak OA, Ruud E (1992). *Den påbegynte virkeligheten: studier i samtidskultur*. Oslo, Norway: Universitetsforlaget.

Berman M (1982). *All that is solid melts into air: the experience of modernity*. New York, NY: Simon & Schuster.

Bjørkvold J-R (1992). *The muse within: creativity and communication, song and play from childhood to maturity*. New York, NY: HarperCollins.

Bjørkvold J-R (1989). *Det musiske mennesket*. Oslo, Norway: Freidig Forlag.

Bollnow OF (1969). *Eksistensfilosofi og pedagogikk*. Oslo, Norway: Fabritius og Sønners Forlag.

Bonny H, Savary L (1973). *Music and your mind: listening with a new consciousness*. London, United Kingdom: Harper & Row.

Bourdieu P (1990). The intellectual field: a world apart. In: *In other words: essays towards a reflexive sociology*. Cambridge, United Kingdom: Polity Press.

Bourdieu P (1984). *Distinction: a social critique of the judgement of taste*. Cambridge, MA: Harvard University Press.

Bråten S (1990). G. H. Mead's filosofi som grunnlag for dialogisk forståelse. In Thuen T, Vaage S (eds): *Oppdragelse til det moderne*. Oslo, Norway: Universitetsforlaget.

Bruscia KE (1995a). Modes of consciousness in Guided Imagery and Music (GIM): a therapist's experience of the guiding process. In Kenny CB (ed): *Listening, playing, creating: essays on the power of sound.* New York, NY: State University of New York Press.

Bruscia KE (1995b). The process of doing qualitative research: part I–III. In Wheeler BL (ed): *Music therapy research: quantitative and qualitative perspectives.* Gilsum, NH: Barcelona Publishers.

Bruscia KE (1994). Authenticity issues in qualitative research. Paper presented at the First International Symposium for Qualitative Research in Music Therapy, Düsseldorf, Germany: July 29–30.

Bruscia KE (1987). *Improvisational models of music therapy.* Springfield, IL: Charles C Thomas.

Buber M (1968). *Jeg og du.* Oslo, Norway: Cappelen.

Chambers I (1990). A miniature history of the Walkman. *New Formations* 11:1–4.

Clynes M (1977). *Sentics, the touch of emotion.* New York, NY: Anchor Press/Doubleday.

Cohen S (1991). *Rock culture in Liverpool: popular music in the making.* Oxford, United Kingdom: Clarendon Press.

Crafts SD, Cavicchi D, Keil C (1993). *My music.* Hanover, Germany: University Press of New England.

Crosby D, Gottlieb C (1988). *Long time gone.* London, United Kingdom: Mandarin.

Dahlhaus C (1978). *Die Idee der absoluten Music.* Kassel, Germany: Bärenreiter-Verlag.

Eckhoff R (1991). Improvisatorisk musikkterapi—del av en integrativ tilnærming i arbeid med tidlig skadete, hospitaliserte, psykiatriske pasienter. In Stige B, Østergaard B (eds): *Le-*

vande musik. Proceedings of the Nordisk Musikkterapikonferanse 1991, Sandane, Norway, May 1–5.

Erikson EH (1968). *Identity, youth and crisis.* New York, NY: W.W. Norton.

Featherstone M (1992). The heroic life and everyday life. In: *Cultural theory and cultural change.* London, United Kingdom: Sage Publications.

Feld S (1988). Aesthetics as iconicity of style, or "lift-up-over sounding": getting into the Kaluli groove. Part 1. *Yearbook for Traditional Music* 20:74–113.

Feld S (1984). Communication, music and speech about music. *Yearbook for Traditional Music* 16:1–18.

Ferrara L (1984). Phenomenology as a tool for musical analysis. *The Musical Quarterly* 70(3):355–373.

Finnegan R (1989). *The hidden musicians: music-making in an English town.* Cambridge, United Kingdom: Cambridge University Press.

Fiske HE (1993). *Music cognition and aesthetic attitudes.* Lewiston, ID: Edwin Mellen Press.

Fiske J (1989a). *Reading the popular.* Boston, MA: Unwin Hyman.

Fiske J (1989a). *Understanding popular culture.* Boston, MA: Unwin Hyman.

Fiske J (1982). *Introduction to communication studies.* London, United Kingdom: Methuen.

Fitzgerald TK (1993). *Metaphors of identity.* New York, NY: State University of New York Press.

Forinash M, Gonzalez D (1989). A phenomenological perspective of music therapy. *Music Therapy* 8:35–46.

Freeman M (1993). *Rewriting the self: history, memory, narrative.* London, United Kingdom: Routledge.

Friedemann L (1974). *Gemeinsame Improvisation auf Instrumenten.* Kassel, Germany: Bärenreiter-Verlag.

Frith S (1996). Music and identity. In Hall S, du Gay P (eds): *1996: questions of cultural identity.* London, United Kingdom: Sage, Publications.

Frith S (1992). The cultural study of popular music. In Grossberg L, Nelson C, Treichler P (eds): *Cultural studies.* New York, NY: Routledge.

Frønes I (1994). *De likeverdige: om sosialisering og de jevnaldrendes betydning.* Oslo, Norway: Universitetsforlaget.

Gabrielsson A, Lindström S (1995). On strong experiences of music. In Steijberg R (ed): *Music and the mind machine: the psychophysiology and psychopathology of the sense of music.* Berlin, Germany: Springer Verlag.

Gabrielsson A, Lindström S (1994). On strong experiences of music. In: *MusikPsychologie, Jahrbuch der Deutschen Gesellschaft für Musikpsychologie.* Vol. 10, 1993.

Gaston ET (1968). *Music in therapy.* New York, NY: Macmillan.

Geertz C (1973). *The interpretation of culture.* New York, NY: Basic Books.

Giddens A (1991). *Modernity and self-identity: self and society in the late modern age.* Cambridge, United Kingdom: Polity Press.

Gilje N (1987). *Hermeneutikk i vitenskapsteoretisk perspektiv.* Senter for vitenskapsteori. Skriftserien nr. 6. Bergen, Norway: Universitetet i Bergen.

Gioia T (1988). *The imperfect art: reflections on jazz and modern culture.* New York, NY: Oxford University Press.

Goffin R (1944). *Jazz: from the Congo to the Metropolitan.* New York, NY: Doubleday. Quoted from Gioia, 1988.

Grootaers F (1983). Improvisation. In Decker-Voigt H-H (ed): *Handbuch Musiktherapie.* Lilienthal/Bremen, Germany: Eres.

Habib HB (1994). *Brain culture and health: towards a preventative theory of health.* Falun, Sweden: Falun Hospital.

Handelman D (1982). Reflexivity in festival and other cultural events. In Douglas M (ed): *Essays on the sociology of perception.* London, United Kingdom: Routledge & Kegan Paul.

Harré R, Gillett G (1994). *The discursive mind.* London, United Kingdom: Sage Publications.

Haug F et al. (1987). *Female sexualization.* London, United Kingdom: Verso.

Hegi F (1986). *Improvisation und Musiktherapie: Möglichkeiten und Wirkungen von freier Musik.* Paderborn, Germany: Junfermann-Verlag.

Hohr H (1990). Lek—kommentar til den kommunikasjonsteoretiske tilnærmingen his Gregory Bateson. *Norsk Pedagogisk Tidsskrift* 2:102–110.

Jacobsen B, Schnack K, Wahlgren, B (1979). *Videnskabsteori.* Copenhagen, Denmark: Gyldendal.

Johns U (1993). Intersubjektivitet som grunnlag for utvikling. *Spesialpedagogikk* 3:41–46.

Josselson R (1994). Identity and relatedness in the life cycle. In Bosma HA, Graafsma TLG, Grotevant HD, de Levita DJ (eds): *Identity and development: an interdisciplinary approach.* London, United Kingdom: Sage Publications.

Jørgensen H (1989). *Musikkopplevelsens psykologi.* Oslo, Norway: Norsk Musikforlag.

Keil C (1987). Participatory discrepancies and the power of music. *Cultural Anthropology* 2(3):275–283.

Keil C (1966). Motion and feeling through music. *Journal of Aesthetics and Art Criticism* 24(3):337–349.

Keil C, Feld S (1994). *Music grooves: essays and dialogues.* Chicago, IL: University of Chicago Press.

Kenny CB (1994). The story of the field of play. Paper presented at the First International Symposium for Qualitative Research in Music Therapy, Düsseldorf, Germany, July 29–30.

Kenny CB (1989). *The field of play: a guide for the theory and practice of music therapy.* Atascadero, CA: Ridgeview Publishing.

Kenny CB (1982). *The mythic artery: the magic of music therapy.* Atascadero, CA: Ridgeview Publishing.

Kleive M, Stige B (1988). Med lengting, liv og song. Oslo, Norway: Samlaget.

Kofsky F (1970). *Black nationalism and the revolution in music.* New York, NY: Pathfinder Press.

Kruse B (1990/91). Improvisasjon—en kreativ prosess. *Opptakt: Informasjonsblad for Norges musikkhøgskole* 2(5)8–11.

Kümmel WF (1977). *Musik und Medizin: Ihre Wechselbeziehungen in Theorie und Praxis von 800 bis 1800.* Freiburg, Germany: Verlag Karl Alber.

Kvale S (1989). In: *Issues of validity in qualitative research.* Lund, Sweden: Studentlitteratur.

Langenberg M, Aigen K, Frommer J, eds. (1996). *Qualitative music therapy research: beginning dialogues,* Gilsum, NH: Barcelona Publishers.

Langenberg M, Frommer J, Langenbach M (1994). Fusion and separation: experiencing opposites in music, music therapy, and music therapy research. Paper presented at the First International Symposium for Qualitative Research in Music Therapy, Düsseldorf, Germany, July 29–30.

Langer S (1953). *Feeling and form.* New York, NY: Charles Scribner's Sons.

Lecourt E (1994). *L'expérience musicale résonances psychanalytiques.* Paris, France: Éditions L'Hartmattan.

Leonard N (1987). *Jazz: myth and religion.* Oxford, United Kingdom: Oxford University Press.

Lewis GH (1995). Taste cultures and musical stereotypes: mirrors of identity? *Popular Music and Society* 19(1):37–58.

Lutz CA (1988). *Unnatural emotions: everyday sentiments on a Micronesian atoll and their challenges to Western theory.* Chicago, IL: University of Chicago Press.

Maslow AH (1968): *Toward a psychology of being.* 2nd ed. New York, NY: Van Nostrand Reinhold.

McClary S (1991). *Feminine endings: music, gender, and sexuality.* Minneapolis, MN: University of Minnesota Press.

Meyer LB (1956). *Emotion and meaning in music.* Chicago, IL: University of Chicago Press.

Middleton R (1990). *Studying popular music.* Milton Keynes, United Kingdom: Open University Press.

Monsen J (1991). *Vitalitet, psykiske forstyrrelser og psykoterapi: Utdrag fra klinisk psykologi.* Oslo, Norway: Tano.

Moreno J (1988). The music therapist: creative arts therapist and contemporary shaman. *The Arts in Psychotherapy* 5:271–280.

Myerhoff B (1990).The transformation of consciousness in ritual performance: some thoughts and questions. In Schechner R, Appel W (eds): *By means of performance: intercultural studies of theatre and ritual*. Cambridge, United Kingdom. Cambridge University Press.

Nordenfelt L (1991a). *Livskvalitet och hälsa: teori och kritik.* Falköping, Sweden: Almquist & Wiksell Förlag.

Nordenfelt L (1991b). *Hälsa och värde.* Stockholm, Sweden: Bokförlaget Thales.

Nordoff P, Robbins C (1977). *Creative Music Therapy.* New York, NY: John Day.

Nordoff P, Robbins C (1971). *Therapy in music for handicapped children.* London, United Kingdom: Victor Gollancz Ltd.

Ølgaard B (1986). *Kommunikation og økomentale systemer ifølge Gregory Bateson.* Åbyhøj, Denmark: Ask.

Østerberg D (1995). Modernitetens estetikk. In Nielsen TV (ed): *Tidens verdier: variasjoner over moral og samfunn.* Oslo, Norway: Universitetsforlaget.

Østerberg D (1988). *Metasociology: an inquiry into the origins and validity of social thought.* Oslo, Norway: Norwegian University Press.

Oversand K (1987). Improvisasjon og tilstedeværelsens estetikk. In Ledang OK (ed): *Musikklidenskapelig.* Oslo, Norway: Solum Forlag.

Panassie H (1971). *Louis Armstrong.* New York, NY: Scribner. Quoted in Gioia, 1988.

Papadakis H (1979). *Epidauros—the sanctuary of Asclepios.* Munich, Germany: Verlag Schnell and Steiner.

Rabinow P (1986). *The Foucault reader.* London, United Kingdom: Penguin.

Rolvsjord R (1996). Et interaksjonsteoretisk perspektiv på musikkterapi. *Musikkterapi* 1:15–30.

Rustøen T (1991). *Livskvalitet: en sykepleieutfordring.* Oslo, Norway: Gyldendal.

Ruud E 1997a. *Musikk og identitet.* Oslo, Norway: Universitetsforlaget.

Ruud E (1996). *Musikk og verdier.* Oslo, Norway: Universitetsforlaget.

Ruud E (1995). Kvalitativ metode i musikkpedagogisk forskning. In Jørgensen H, Hanken IM (eds): *Nordisk musikkpedagogisk forskning.* Oslo, Norway: State Academy of Music Publication.

Ruud E (1992a). Improvisasjon som liminal erfaring—om jazz og musikkterapi som overgangsritualer. In Berkaak OA, Ruud E: *Den påbegynte virkeligheten: studier i samtidskultur.* Oslo, Norway: Universitetsforlaget.

Ruud E (1992b). Metropolens lydspor. In Berkaak OA, Ruud, E: *Den påbegynte virkeligheten: studier i samtidskultur.* Oslo, Norway: Universitetsforlaget.

Ruud E (1991). Musikalsk stil som emosjonell diskurs. *Studia Musicologica Norvegica* 17:137–169.

Ruud E (1990a). *Musikk som kommunikasjon og samhandling.* Oslo, Norway: Solum.

Ruud E (1990b). *Caminos da musicoterapia.* São Paulo, Brazil: Summus Editorial.

Ruud E (1990c). *Los Caminos de la musicoterapia* Buenos Aires, Argentina: Summus Editorial.

Ruud E (1989). Musica come communicazione. *Bolletino Semestrale d'Informazione* (AISMt.) 1–2:11–15.

Ruud E (1987). Musikk som kommunikasjon og samhandling. Doctoral dissertation. Oslo, Norway: Universitetet i Oslo.

Ruud E (1986). Music as communication—a perspective from semiotics and communication theory. In: *Music and health*. Oslo, Norway: Norsk Musikforlag.

Ruud E (1980a). *Hva er musikkterapi?* Oslo, Norway: Gyldendal.

Ruud E (1980b). *Music therapy and its relationship to current treatment theories.* St. Louis, MO: Magnamusic Baton.

Ruud E (1978). *Musikkterapi—en oversikt.* Oslo, Norway: Norsk Musikforlag.

Ruud E (1975). Om mål og midler i musikkterapien. *Musikkterapinytt* 2/3:4–10.

Ruud E, Mahns W (1991). *Meta-Musiktherapie.* Stuttgart, Germany: Gusrav Fischer Verlag.

Ruud E, Stige B (1994). Erfaringer fra musikkterapi som modell for en ny tenkning rundt forholdet mellom kultur og helse. In Irjala A (ed): *Kultur gär hälsa. Proceedings of the Nordisk konferanse.* Esbo, Finland.

Sachs L (1993). Hälsa som kultur: en antropologs funderinger. In Philipson S, Uddenberg N (eds): *Hälsa som livsmening.* Borås, Sweden: Natur och kultur.

Schultz EA, Lavenda RH (1990): *Cultural anthropology: a perspective on the human condition.* St. Paul, MN: West Publishing.

Schütz A (1951). Making music together. *Social Research* 18:76–97.

Shepherd J (1993). Value and power in music. In Blundell V, Shepherd J, Taylor I (eds): *Relocating cultural studies. developments in theory and research.* London, United Kingdom: Routledge.

Siggaard Jensen H (1986). Music and health in post-modern society. In Ruud E (ed): *Music and health.* Oslo, Norway: Norsk Musikforlag.

Sinding-Larsen H (1984). Landskappleiken—nasjonalt rituale og lokalkulturell folkefest. In Klausen AM (ed): *Den norske væremåten.* Oslo, Norway: Cappelen.

Smeijsters H (1997). *Multiple perspectives: a guide to qualitative research in music therapy.* Gilsum, NH: Barcelona Publishers.

Smeijsters H (1994). Qualitative single-case research in practice: a necessary, reliable, and valid alternative for music therapy research. Paper presented at the First International Symposium for Qualitative Research in Music Therapy, Düsseldorf, Germany, July 29–30.

Stefani G, ed. (1996). *Intense emozioni in musica.* Bologna, Italy: Cooperativa Libraria Editrice Universitaria Bologna.

Stefani G (1989). Cultura musical per la pace. In: *Musica con coscienza.* Turin, Italy: Edizioni Paoline.

Stern D (1996). Temporal aspects of an infant's daily experience: some reflections concerning music. Keynote address at the 8th World Congress of Music Therapy, Hamburg, Germany, July 18.

Stern D (1991). *Barnets interpersonelle univers.* Copenhagen, Denmark: Hans Reitzels Forlag.

Stige B (1996). Music, music therapy, and health promotion. In *Culture and health: report from the international confer-*

ence on culture and health. Oslo, Norway: Norwegian National Commission for UNESCO, September 28–30, 1995.

Stige B (1995). *Samspel og relasjon.* Oslo, Norway: Samlaget.

Stokes M, ed. (1994). *Ethnicity, identity and music: the musical construction of place.* Oxford, United Kingdom: Berg.

Strauss A, Corbin J (1990). *Basics of qualitative research: grounded theory procedures and techniques.* London, United Kingdom: Sage Publications.

Taylor C (1995). *The ethics of authenticity.* Cambridge, MA: Harvard University Press.

Turner Victor (1974). *Dramas, fields, and metaphors: symbolic action in human society.* Ithaca, NY: Cornell University Press.

Turner V (1969). *The ritual process: structure and antistructure.* Ithaca, NY: Cornell University Press.

Tüpker R (1990). Wissenschaftlichkeit in kunsttherapeutischer Forschung. *Musiktherapeutische Umschau* 11:7–20.

Tüpker R (1988). *Ich singe, was ich nicht sagen kann: Zu einer morphologischen Grundlegung der Musiktherapie.* Regensburg, Germany: Gustav Bosse Verlag.

Walser R (1995). "Out of notes": signification, interpretation, and the problem of Miles Davis. In Gabbard K (ed): *Jazz among the discourses.* Durham, NC: Duke University Press.

Waterman CA (1990). *Juju: a social history and ethnography of an African popular music.* Chicago, IL: University of Chicago Press.

Watzlawick P (1976). *How real is real? Confusion, disinformation, communication.* New York, NY: Vintage Books.

Wheeler BL, ed. (1995). *Music therapy research: quantitative and qualitative perspectives.* Gilsum, NH: Barcelona Publishers.

Widdershoven, GAM (1993). The story of life: hermeneutic perspectives on the relationship between narrative and life history. In Josselson R, Lieblich A (eds): *The narrative study of lives.* London, United Kingdom: Sage Publications.

Wikshåland S (1995). Beethoven-variasjoner. In Gundersen K, Wikshåland S (eds): *Gåter: Grunnlagsproblemer i estetisk forskning.* Vol. XI. Oslo, Norway: Norges forskningsråd.

Willis P (1990). *Common culture.* Milton Keynes, United Kingdom: Open University Press.

Wittgenstein L (1967). *Philosophical investigations.* 3rd ed. Oxford, United Kingdom: Basil Blackwell.

Wrangsjö B (1994). När själven möts uppstår musik—Daniel Stern's självteori. *Nordic Journal of Music Therapy* 3(2):79–83.

Yalom ID (1997). *Kjærlighetens bøddel og andre terapeutiske fortellinger.* Oslo, Norway: Pax.

INDEX